THE UPSTART GUIDE TO

OWNING AND MANAGING

BAR OR TAVERN

SECOND EDITION

ROY S. ALONZO

KAPLAN) PUBLISHING

President, Kaplan Publishing: Roy Lipner
Vice President and Publisher: Maureen McMahon
Acquisitions Editor: Michael Cunningham
Development Editor: Trey Thoelcke
Production Editor: Karen Goodfriend
Typesetters: Todd Bowman, Janet Schroeder
Cover Designer: KTK Design

Published by Kaplan Publishing,
a division of Kaplan, Inc.

Printed in the United States of America

06 07 08 10 9 8 7 6 5 4 3 2 1

Library of Congress Cataloging-in-Publication Data

Alonzo, Roy S.
   The upstart guide to owning and managing a bar or tavern / Roy S. Alonzo. —2nd ed.
      p. cm.
   Includes bibliographical references and index.
   ISBN-13: 978-1-4195-3553-6 (alk. paper)
   ISBN-10: 1-4195-3553-6 (alk. paper)
   1. Bars (Drinking establishments)—Management. 2. Taverns (Inns)—Management. I. Title.
   TX950.7.A49 2006
   647.95068—dc22

                                                          2006011619

Kaplan Publishing books are available at special quantity discounts to use for sales promotions, employee premiums, or educational purposes. Please call our Special Sales Department to order or for more information at 800-621-9621, ext. 4444, e-mail *kaplanpubsales@kaplan.com,* or write to Kaplan Publishing, 30 South Wacker Drive, Suite 2500, Chicago, IL 60606-7481.

DEDICATION

I sincerely thank my wife Darlene, to whom I dedicate this book, for her cheerful encouragement.

The very favorable response to the first edition of this book showed there is an ongoing need for guidance on the process of starting up, owning, and managing a bar or tavern. The technological innovations, and population and behavioral changes of the past decade, along with new millennium trends, prompted this second edition.

Remember the last time you were in a bar, having a great time and enjoying good drinks and food with convivial friends? Did the thought cross your mind that it was a wonderful bar and you admiringly wished it were yours? If you have an entrepreneurial bent, that would not have been an uncommon thought. Most of us are attracted by the places we like, especially if they appear to be highly profitable.

This book is intended to give you a sense of what the bar business is like and to help you evaluate whether it is the right business for you. For those who conclude it is, this book will help you navigate through the process of starting up or buying and successfully managing such a venture. Although the basics of the business have not changed over the past decade, the way bars and taverns are marketed has changed, as has the equipment used, the products sold, the laws regulating the industry, and the way business is conducted.

Today's bars are not just selling drinks, they are selling atmosphere, entertainment, a social experience, interesting food, relaxation for some and excitement for others, and, hopefully, a memorable experience that will generate valued word-of-mouth advertising.

The opening chapters will give you a background of the industry and insights into current trends that are shaping the business. The following chapters will then guide you through the process of starting a bar—from the initial idea to the grand opening—and give you techniques and procedures for operating it profitably. The contents are supported with examples, checklists, and action guidelines. This book is as much a source for business-building ideas as it is a roadmap for getting through the start-up process. The appendixes include a sample business plan and up-to-date lists of contact information for state regulatory agencies.

While this book is not intended to make you an expert in accounting, law, architecture, or other specialized fields, it will give you an awareness of what is involved in all areas of the bar business, and will allow you to effectively communicate your wishes and concerns to the professionals with whom you may deal.

Laws vary from state to state and between various levels of government. Where any laws are discussed in this book, it is only to make you aware of their existence. Consequently, nothing in this book is offered as legal advice or an interpretation of a law and should not be construed as such. Information of that kind should be obtained from an attorney and the appropriate government officials, as should advice on accounting matters be sought from specialized professionals.

The mention of any product names in this book is done merely for illustrative purposes and should not be deemed an endorsement. Likewise, where products are mentioned, the omission of any particular products is not in any way a reflection on such products.

Finally, this book is intended to stimulate thinking about the bar and tavern business, to answer a variety of questions, and to present an assortment of management tools that may be used to successfully operate a bar or tavern. To those who may someday become proprietors of a bar, tavern, nightclub, or restaurant, we wish you a full measure of success and happiness in your quest to achieve your goals.

The contributions of many people and companies helped make this book possible. I would like to thank the Perlick Corporation, and in particular Scott Schloerke, for information, photos, and drawings; Peter Egleston for sharing the history of the Portsmouth Brewery and the Smuttynose Brewing Company and for information on microbreweries; Redhook Brewery and Ryan Berry for photos; Joseph Danehy of the University of New Hampshire for his computer expertise; Barbara Balboni, editor at R.S. Means Publishing Co.; Nancy Urtz, reference librarian at St. Anselm's College; the University of New Hampshire Reference Library staff; Karin Witmer of the National Restaurant Association—Educational Foundation; Chad Hale of Perkins Equipment Inc., for equipment information; Datamonitor for information on megatrends; the Massachusetts Liquor Commission for information on the liquor laws of that state; and the New Hampshire Liquor Commission for information on the liquor laws of that state. I would also like to thank Larry Levine and Schramsberg Vineyards of Calistoga, CA, for photos; Ron Potter and Motoman, a Yaskawa Company for the use of photos; the Library Restaurant for photos, Kenneth Roberts, photographer; and Michael Cunningham, my editor at Kaplan Publishing, for his support.

1

THE BAR BUSINESS

A bar—it's a place to relax with your favorite beverage, a place to meet friends and enjoy good conversation or music. There are bars that sell food and restaurants that sell alcoholic beverages. There are wine bars, brewpubs, sports bars, club bars, the list goes on. Today, a bar can be any of these things, but it wasn't always that way.

In colonial times, a tavern was defined as a place that "provided food, drink, and lodging for man and his beast," and their establishment was often decreed by law to assist in advancing the frontiers. Now, a generally accepted definition of a bar or tavern is a licensed business where alcoholic beverages are sold to be consumed on the premises. Beyond that, each state and local government has its own specific requirements for the various types of licenses it issues.

In recent years, a greater awareness of alcohol responsibility has changed drinking habits. Today, most people do not go to bars just to drink; they go to bars for many reasons: To meet other people, to conduct business or eat while drinking, to dance or listen to music, or to watch sporting events and other entertainment. Consequently, most bars are linked with other activities, and an establishment's identification in the public's view is largely a function of how its management chooses to position it in the marketplace and what its greatest source of revenue is.

A LONG AND HONORABLE HISTORY

Alcoholic beverages have deep roots in American history. Licenses were held by many honorable men: pillars of the church, leaders of the community, and political and military figures. Taverns were often the secret meeting places of such prominent patriots as George Washington, Benjamin Franklin, Thomas Jefferson, Paul Revere, and Sam and John Adams during the early revolutionary days. After the Revolutionary War, George Washington distilled whiskey and Sam Adams was a brewer. Abraham Lincoln held a tavern license in Springfield, Illinois. Since then, much has changed, but the bar and tavern business continues to thrive.

Prior to the Prohibition era, the food and beverage industry had very few management controls. Liquor profits were sufficiently high as to disinterest proprietors from spending a great deal of time or effort on controls. Management was conducted to a large extent by whim and personality, rather than systems and procedures. When the Prohibition Act was implemented in 1920, the manufacture and sale of alcoholic beverages was outlawed. Many proprietors panicked at the thought of having to survive with only food sales.

The large companies took action to protect their investments. They engaged accountants to study their operations and recommend ways to operate their food businesses profitably. The accountants compared the food service industry to other industries and concluded it had many similarities. Other industries have three basic spheres of activity: 1) procurement and warehousing, 2) manufacturing, and 3) sales and service. The food and beverage industry has the same three, called by different names: food and beverage purchasing and storage, food and beverage production (cooking and bartending), and sales and table service.

When viewed that way, it became obvious that the same kinds of accountability and controls used by industry in general could be adapted to the food and beverage industry. That was done, and the industry not only survived, it profited. After the Prohibition Act was repealed in 1933, legalizing the sale of liquor, the question arose: "Do we go back to the old ways, or continue to use accounting controls?" The answer was clearly to continue with controls and to expand them to the liquor side of the business as well. That was the birth of beverage controls as we know them today.

FIGURE 1.1   *The Intimate Bar at the Library Restaurant, Portsmouth, New Hampshire*

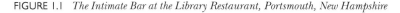

Photo by Ken Roberts

Hotel companies, restaurant chains, the National Restaurant Association, and institutions of higher education that offer hospitality programs have been the most active in developing management systems and control procedures. However, even with a developed state of the art, many independent beverage operations still function without adequate controls, a shortcoming this book will address.

For the person seeking an attractive return on investment, the bar and tavern business offers opportunities and challenges. It must, however, be run in a businesslike manner and utilize the same management practices and controls required for any successful business. The owner of a bar or tavern must have a keen sense of market savvy. Knowledge of one's guests' wants and needs is critical to success.

SO YOU WANT TO BE IN THE BAR BUSINESS

Most people have enjoyable memories of their experiences in bars. So much so that some decide to enter the beverage business for a livelihood. There is a great attraction to the bar business: The chance to meet interesting people, to work in a social atmosphere, and to be with people having fun. These are strong attractions, but should not be principal reasons for entering the business.

NOT FOR EVERYONE

Not everyone who likes to eat out should be in the restaurant business. The same applies to bars. Bars have excellent profit-making potential when they are properly run, but they also require long hours, painstaking attention to details, working on weekends and holidays, and sometimes putting up with nuisance guests. These are the realities of the business, and you cannot expect to have a successful operation without being willing to endure these hardships. Increasingly, we find other professional and commercial people—pilots, police officers, fire fighters, doctors and nurses, as well as people in the retailing and service fields— also working odd hours, weekends, and holidays. The redeeming feature of the bar business is it offers the opportunity for substantial profits.

The bar business is one that people like or dislike, and those who like it seem to love it—even with its unusual characteristics. A well-managed, ethically run beverage business can offer a high degree of job satisfaction. It also can render prestige to its owners in the form of social acceptance and public recognition.

PROFILE OF A SUCCESSFUL START-UP

The old saying that *good ideas aren't worth a dime unless they are acted upon* is true—most people's good ideas simply fade away. But not so for Peter Egleston, owner of the Portsmouth Brewery and Smuttynose Brewing Company. He acted on one idea so fast that he became a brewing company owner by the end of the day.

Midway between a large hotel, three picturesque tugboats docked side-by-side in the harbor, and bustling Market Square with its pastries, lattes, and sidewalk tables, is the Portsmouth Brewery, a pub-type restaurant in seacoast New Hampshire. It serves an array of handcrafted beers and ales and offers a four-page menu of café food with something for every palate. Walk in, and you'll quickly know why it is successful. Everything about this restaurant is done with its guests in mind. Across the city is the Smuttynose Brewing Company. It makes the handcrafted beers and ales that are served at the restaurant, and which are now distributed from New England to Virginia.

It all started when Egleston's sister, Janet, moved back east from California and told him about the brewpubs that were gaining popularity there. Being fond of beer and ale, the idea of handcrafting them intrigued him, so together as partners they opened one of the first brewpubs in the northeast, the Northampton Brewery, in 1987 in Massachusetts.

Outfitting a brewpub was not easy in those days. Egleston rummaged around the country searching for used tanks and pumps and other fixtures and equipment necessary to make beer. He finally wound up having all new equipment fabricated by a manufacturer in Portland, Oregon, using bank loans and personal savings.

The time was right for starting a brewpub, people were becoming educated in the unique qualities of well-crafted beers and ales, and many switched to them from other alcoholic beverages. Banking on his knowledge of making home brew, and occasionally tapping experts for help, Egleston did all of the brewing for the first few years. Before long, the Northampton Brewery was a viable enterprise.

Fueled by that success, Egleston and his sister decided to open a second brewpub when they learned of the availability of a prime location in New Hampshire. The Portsmouth Brewery opened in 1991, and for a number of years they maintained a presence in the two locations, with each commuting back and forth every week. That model was difficult to sustain and both businesses suffered from lack of focus, a situation that would be remedied.

The Brewery, as it is commonly called, draws an eclectic clientele consisting of merchants, retail employees, professionals, tourists, local residents, theater-goers, and celebrators of all kinds of special occa-

FIGURE 1.2   *The Portsmouth Brewery, a Brewpub Restaurant in Portsmouth, New Hampshire*

Photo courtesy of Peter Egleston, owner

sions, including blizzards. Guests have been known to arrive on cross-country skis, knowing the Brewery stays open when many other establishments are closed.

Drawn by its reputation for serving fine handcrafted beers and ales, and its menu that offers a wide range of choices, the Brewery's core clientele comes for various reasons—lunch, dinner, after work relaxation, or an evening out. The pub is abuzz with sound on crowded nights, standing room only at the bar, yet its multilevel floor plan allows guests to carry on normal conversations in booths.

The Brewery's menu includes unique appetizers, both light and hearty sandwiches, soups and salads, and an interesting variety of dinners priced from $10.95 to $21.95. The menu items are prepared from fresh ingredients to the greatest extent possible.

Egleston takes pride in the fact that the Brewery, which has a full bar that serves wines and liquors in addition to its flagship beers and ales, stocks only *call brands* in its wells. That means every drink is made with a well-known, quality product. He also tries to change the wine list three or four times a year to enable his guests to enjoy new wine experiences. He attributes the success of the Brewery to his determination to stick to it, and to his overriding belief that a business must put its guests first. "Business has to be earned," he says, "it doesn't come easy. I try to consider the long term when making decisions."

In 1993, Egleston learned about a soon to occur bank auction of the assets of a bankrupt small brewing company. He went to the auction simply out of curiosity, but came home the sole owner of a building full of equipment. In effect, he had just entered the wider world of microbrewing. That was the beginning of what would be named the Smuttynose Brewing Company.

It took about nine months to get the system back into working order, test new batches, design and print packaging, and assemble a distribution network. In mid-1994, he shipped out his first cases of Smuttynose Ale, and soon followed up with four other products, including Old Brown Ale, named after his dog.

Swept up by the 1990's boom that produced massive sales increases in the microbrewing industry, some microbreweries rushed to increase their production capacity at considerable cost in order to meet demand. At the same time, new microbreweries were popping up all around the country and some, unfortunately, produced products of less than expected quality. That, coupled with rising imports of foreign beers and ales, caused the demand to suddenly level off, and many microbreweries failed. Egleston's Smuttynose Brewing Company avoided that demise by sticking to its strategy of producing quality products and concentrating on building a strong regional market.

After 15 years, Egleston and his sister ended their business partnership in 2001. Janet became the sole owner of the Northampton Brewery and Egleston now focuses his entire attention on the Portsmouth Brewery and Smuttynose Brewing Company.

Smuttynose beer has won gold medals at the Great British Beer Festival, and most recently its Wheat Wine Ale won a gold medal at the 2005 Great American Beer Festival competition in Denver, Colorado. Sales of its beers and ales have increased dramatically over the past few years, the company is earning profits, and Egleston is optimistic about the future: "It's still about quality and pleasing the guest."

A TYPICAL DAY IN A MANAGER'S LIFE

An owner/manager of a bar can wear many hats in the course of a day. How many will depend on his or her particular skills and interests and the size of the establishment. In a large operation, many duties are to be delegated to office managers and other staff people, but in a small start-up business, monetary constraints usually require owners to do many things themselves.

A typical day could include checking the previous days receipts and preparing the bank deposit, inventorying the bar and ordering stock, preparing work schedules, working on the payroll, talking to salespeople, interviewing applicants for jobs, placing advertisements with media representatives, conducting meetings with employees, repairing a broken piece of equipment, checking out food and drink prices, planning new menu items, working up sales promotion ideas, checking on the quality of products and guest service, and working the floor to meet and greet the clientele.

Few jobs present such a broad variety of challenges and allow a person to exercise so great a range of skills. One thing is certain in the bar business—it is never boring.

CAN SOMEONE ELSE MANAGE FOR YOU?

Yes, provided the person is knowledgeable about the liquor business, honest, dedicated, and willing to make the same kind of personal sacrifices that you would be willing to make. The degree to which such a person may succeed will depend largely on the motivation and system of rewards you give.

IS BAR OWNERSHIP FOR YOU?

The bar business is an entrepreneurial experience and as such has risks, disappointments, seemingly endless demands for time and money, and no surefire guarantee of success. Some people thrive on challenges, which bring out their best qualities. Others feel insecure and uncomfortable when faced with uncertainty. Are you cut out to be an entrepreneur?

Are you willing to risk your savings for a business? Are you amenable to a second mortgage on your house and borrowing from friends and relatives? Are you willing and able to work 12 hours or more a day, 7 days a week, if necessary? Can you tolerate the uncertainty that might prevail during the infant years of the business? Can you stand the pressure of being the leader and shouldering the responsibility of keeping a business afloat when all others may have given up? Are you willing to forgo your social life and very likely your vacation during the start-up period, which may be protracted?

The answers to these questions are an indication of your passion for small business. Most people prefer the stability of a 9-to-5 job with a steady paycheck, and there is absolutely nothing wrong with that. But, if you are the type of person who thrives on seeing your creation grow, in spite of the sacrifices required, then being in business for yourself may be an exhilarating and profitable experience for you.

Action **G**uidelines

- ✓ Give yourself an entrepreneurial test to determine your tolerance for business risks.
- ✓ Identify your goals and list your priorities to determine whether the bar business would give you the satisfaction you seek.
- ✓ List your skills and interests and assess how closely they match up to those required or useful in the bar business.
- ✓ Talk to people in the business in noncompeting markets, and get the benefit of their knowledge and advice.
- ✓ Read books and trade publications on the alcoholic beverage industry to become acquainted with the field.

2

CHANGE
AND INNOVATION

THE NATURE OF CHANGE

We live in a rapidly changing society—human behavior is changing, so are our institutions—and the hospitality field is no exception. Anyone who starts up a bar or tavern business today should be aware of the trends that are affecting the industry and that will continue to shape it in the near future. We must recognize that change is inevitable; we can either resist it or adapt to it. History shows us that businesses that step up and embrace change, or innovate ways to cope with it, are better able to manage their outcomes and often find opportunities in them. Chapters 3 through 14 will guide you through the start-up process, but first let's look at the nature of change and some current trends that are having an impact on the bar business.

More and more, it requires creativity to flourish in the bar business. Fewer people go out just to drink. With faster-paced lives and a craving for more intense levels of satisfaction, people want their going-out experience to include other attractions, such as good food, music, dancing, entertainment, an opportunity to meet people, gambling where permitted, and, for some, an intimate ambiance that encourages conversation. Different people have different desires and needs, and technology companies have raced to fill those needs with creative solutions in every area of the business, from high-tech sound and lighting systems that can capture any mood to electronic games that entertain and Wi-Fi networks that allow people to be productive while relaxing. Some of the changes that are shaping the bar and tavern business include the following:

- Greater use of the Internet to find information on bars and restaurants, including their menus, location and directions, hours of business, and entertainment offered
- New legislation regarding intoxication while driving, and growing pressures from the public for responsible drinking
- The introduction of computer technology to almost all aspects of the business
- The continuing trend of busy working people toward casual dining, healthier foods, grazing in bars, and the increasing popularity of cocktails among younger adults
- The education of servers of alcoholic beverages on responsibility issues
- The development of new products, such as flavored beers (malternatives) and liquors, and labor-saving equipment
- The growing popularity of games for entertainment and games of chance

Technology companies have developed products for the hospitality field that make jobs less tiresome and increase profits. Handheld devices and computer software have been designed to take the tedium out of such tasks as taking inventory, and other automated machines take the drudgery out of pot washing and the cleaning of floors and restrooms, jobs that have a high labor turnover rate.

Liquor-dispensing systems that function in concert with a bartender have been available for some time, but now at least one company has developed a robotic bar system where a robot can make drinks by itself. The robotic bartender is claimed to increase profits by eliminating spillage, making drinks accurately and quickly, and increasing volume by generating interest.

One of the trademarks of successful businesses is their ability to recognize emerging trends and determine the wants and needs of the public that will result from their outcomes. If businesses are to maintain their

FIGURE 2.1 *RoboBar Automatically Makes Cocktails and Pours Beer, Wine, and Soft Drinks*

Photo courtesy of Motoman, a Yaskawa Company

market position or, in some cases, survive, they must be alert to what is happening around them.

Datamonitor, a global market analysis firm, has identified ten mega-trends that are expected to affect new products and services in the near future—convenience, health, age complexity, gender complexity, life-stage complexity, income complexity, individualism, sensory, comfort, and connectivity.

One may extrapolate implications of such trends and identify the challenges and opportunities that they will present to the hospitality industry. Bar and restaurant owners must examine all aspects of their businesses to find ways to make it easier, faster, healthier, and more appealing and satisfying for people to patronize their establishments. Let's take a closer look at these ten trends:

1. *Convenience.* Time-saving products are now important to 82 percent of American and European consumers. The challenge: How can you make your products and services more accessible to your target clientele?

2. *Health.* Ninety percent of American and European consumers feel that improving their health is important. The challenge: How can you offer healthy choices to this large market segment?

3. *Age complexity.* Younger consumers are acquiring more spending power and developing brand awareness and loyalty at an earlier age. The challenge: How can you keep up with the brands your clientele want?

4. *Gender complexity.* Gender roles are less defined than ever before. The challenge: How can you broaden your market appeal?

5. *Life-stage complexity.* While the nuclear family staying together through life is still the norm in most countries, it is changing. The challenge: How can you be ready to serve new needs? Even the pubs in England and Ireland are changing.

6. *Income complexity.* Lower-income and mid-market consumers are increasingly seeking luxury on a budget. The challenge: How can you upgrade to make your bar appear more lavish?

7. *Individualism.* The large increase in the number of *single* consumers is reflected in spending patterns that match their attitudes and outlook on life. The challenge: How can you ensure that your seating and table arrangements are welcoming to singles?

8. *Sensory.* Consumers are seeking out more intense experiences from products and services and are more willing to experiment with new ones. The challenge: How can you consider what guests see, hear, and touch, when making decisions about your bar? How can you match their wants and expectations?

9. *Comfort.* Consumers appear to be increasingly seeking comfort foods, to enjoy small indulgences and escape the pressures of daily life. The challenge: How can you give guests choices that satisfy those needs?

10. *Connectivity.* The growth in ethnic consumption reflects a need to connect, and is about community belonging and sharing values and attitudes. The challenge: How can you keep the opportunities associated with this trend from slipping by?

Capitalizing on these trends is important to businesses seeking to grow. Shifting behavioral patterns, such as young people marrying at older ages, middle-agers being more open to youthful trends, and older people living longer and defying stereotypical myths, will certainly affect consumption patterns.

Datamonitor produces comprehensive analytical reports on these and other trends, and can be found online at *www.datamonitor.com*. The National Restaurant Association also informs its members on industry changes and trends through its newsletter, *SmartBriefs,* its annual Restaurant Industry Operations Report, and its Educational Foundation publications.

PROBLEM-SOLVING INNOVATIONS

Innovations are popping up as fast as problems can be identified, making true the adage, *one person's problem is another person's opportunity.* New products reaching the marketplace range from small gadgets to large equipment, and elaborate electronic systems that integrate many activities of a business.

With faster-paced lifestyles today, anything that speeds up service is a welcomed innovation for many people. Few things vex diners and drinkers more than having to wait to pay their bill, especially if they are in a hurry and are paying with a credit card. That problem has been solved by wireless technology. Several companies have developed handheld wireless credit card terminals that can handle the task of cashiering tableside in a fraction of the time it would otherwise take. The waitperson simply swipes the guest's card through the small device, and it authorizes the transaction in seconds. The device then produces a printed receipt that the guest signs, along with a copy. That's it.

The advantages of this innovation are it eliminates calling in credit cards by phone or walking back and forth to swipe the card on a stationary terminal, they print clear and reliable receipts, information can be downloaded to other computer programs, there may be lower processing fees charged by some credit card companies, and guests like the idea that their credit card does not leave their sight. In addition, it gives the bar or restaurant a favorable image, one of being on the cutting edge and successful.

Another innovation that bars and restaurants are beginning to offer is a Wi-Fi hotspot. Wi-Fi, which stands for Wireless Fidelity, is a technology that allows mobile devices, such as laptop computers and personal digital assistants, to connect to the Internet from within a local area network. This feature is particularly attractive to people who work with computers and wish to make their visit to a bar or restaurant a productive or entertaining experience. Some establishments offer Wi-Fi access for a fee, others offer it for free. It is an increasingly popular feature for sidewalk cafés and venues with courtyard seating to offer, and engenders highly desirable word-of-mouth advertising as people spread the word.

Electronic beer-keg gauging equipment is a new innovation that permits the continuous measuring of the contents of kegs in action. It measures the amount of beer dispensed, as well as the amount of beer remaining in a keg. This allows for better timing of keg changeovers at busy times, and eliminates guessing the contents of partially full kegs.

The days of the plain bar, with stools and a few booths, are numbered. People seek bars with distinctive décors and an ambiance that will transport their minds to a different place. Décors based on almost any theme imaginable are more obtainable now than ever before. They can be built on-site or purchased in their entirety, complete with authentic details and wall hangings, from firms that specialize in the business. English and Irish pubs are built abroad, and can be purchased through agents in the United States. The component sections are dismantled for shipping to the United States, and reassembled at the buyer's site. Contact information for such manufacturers can be found in architectural directories and at restaurant and bar trade shows.

Handheld devices are replacing the pen and guest check book. Waitpersons can take food and beverage orders and then transmit them wirelessly tableside to the kitchen or bar. This saves time for the waitperson, speeds up service for guests, and reduces traffic to the bar and kitchen. The digital devices may contain food and liquor menus with descriptive details on each, which allow servers to answer questions immediately and to offer suggestions. They also provide a trail for tracking orders. The devices are most useful in fast-paced, high-volume establishments.

Gift certificate giving has been enhanced by the availability of digital gift cards that resemble credit cards in size but are monogrammed with the name and logo of the issuer and are only usable at that establishment or chain. In addition to being convenient for guests to carry in their wallet, they can provide the seller with three types of information: gift card sales, redemptions, and outstanding balances. They are a significant improvement over traditional paper gift certificates that, when not properly handled, can cause embarrassing problems regarding unused balances, and are less secure.

Guest paging systems are another innovation that continues to grow in popularity. They allow guests waiting to be seated in a dining room to do so at the bar, and thereby reduce crowding at the host's stand. They also alleviate the problem of finding people who are in restrooms or may have stepped outside to make a cell phone call or smoke when paged. They are a welcomed change from the blare of a host calling *the Jones party for two* over a microphone.

Newer and better inventory control systems that feature handheld devices can scan the bar code on liquor bottles as the bottles are weighed on an electronic scale. They then report the results to an office computer, where sales are reconciled with liquor usage and inventories are updated. These innovations make bar control much easier and more accurate.

Automatic pot washing machines with booster heaters, high-pressure nozzles, and roll-in carts can take the drudgery out of that unpopular job. They are equipped with all the necessary features to meet National Sanitation Foundation (NSF) standards.

Point of sale (POS) systems that integrate the activities of the front of the house with those of the back of the house and the office continue to grow in use. They are constantly being improved to do more things, be easier to use, and be tailored to the specific needs of a business. POS systems capture data on touch-screen terminals at the time and place that an order is taken, and transmit the information to the kitchen, cashiering, and to other computer systems, such as inventorying, that are affected by the transaction.

Changes and innovations will continue to affect all aspects of the industry, and we can expect them to occur at an increasingly faster pace as technological capabilities multiply. Our challenge is to adapt to the changes, ride the waves, and not be swept along aimlessly or left behind.

Action **G**uidelines

✓ Visit trade shows to learn about new equipment and other products; in particular, the Bar and Nightclub Show and the National Restaurant Show.

✓ Visit food and beverage equipment dealerships and talk to salespeople to learn about new products and solutions to problems.

✓ Subscribe to trade magazines, and keep abreast of events and trends that may impact your business.

3

START-UP
REQUIREMENTS

As with all entrepreneurial start-ups, the bar business has certain requirements, but because it involves the sale of alcoholic beverages, it is also a licensed and governmentally regulated business. Its requirements can be categorized as financial, personal, location, and governmental.

FINANCIAL REQUIREMENTS

When determining the financial needs of your proposed venture, you must consider every aspect of the preopening activities that will require money. The amounts will of course vary with the size and scope of the business you have in mind, but none should be overlooked. In general, you will need finances for the following three initial stages of your project:

1. *Initial planning.* This includes accounting and legal resources; market research; and general expenses, such as telephone, duplicating, transportation, acquisition of licenses and permits, etc.
2. *Construction and acquisition of equipment.* This includes building or renovating the facility, purchasing and installing the necessary equipment and furnishings, and obtaining the appropriate operating supplies and inventories.

3. *Preopening expenses and working capital.* This includes cleaning up after construction, advertising, hiring and training staff, and having adequate funds to meet payroll and pay other bills until your cash flow builds to where it can sustain current operational costs.

For initial planning purposes, you can obtain interior cost estimates from a book titled *Means Interiors Cost Data.* Division 11 of that book contains estimates for commercial kitchen and bar equipment, and division 12 contains estimates on furnishings. If you are considering erecting a building to house your project, cost estimates can be obtained on a per-seat or a square-footage basis from another book published by R.S. Means Co. titled *Means Building Construction Cost Data.* Both books may be ordered through bookstores, or online at *www.contractor-books.com,* however, a copy might be available for research at your local library.

SOURCES OF FINANCING

To a great degree, you must depend on your own resources, partners, or investors. Most financial institutions won't lend money for new food or beverage operations unless the borrower has adequate collateral to make the loan virtually risk free. This is due to tight banking policies and the historically high failure rate in the industry. In any case, lenders and investors will look at your capital, collateral, and character.

PERSONAL REQUIREMENTS

The personal skills required of an owner of a bar are largely determined by how active he or she wishes to become. Bartending skills are useful when an employee does not show up on time and during unexpected rush periods. Basic accounting skills are also helpful, both for understanding the books and for filling in when the bookkeeper is on vacation.

What it comes down to is an owner can pay other people to do the tasks that need to be performed, or the owner may personally do some things. The motivation for owner involvement is usually to save money or to keep a tighter control on operations.

Following is a list of sources of funds, including some that are often overlooked:

- Personal savings
- Taking in partners
- Incorporating
- Cash value of life insurance policies
- Loans from relatives
- Loans from friends
- Collateralized bank loans
- Credit terms from equipment suppliers
- Credit from food suppliers
- Finance companies

In addition to skill requirements, there are attitude requirements. An owner of a bar should truly enjoy serving the public, and employees must believe that satisfying the clientele is the uppermost priority of a bar. Owners must be persistent in their training and supervision to communicate this message to the staff.

LOCATION REQUIREMENTS

A bar must be accessible to its target market. If it caters to business-people at noontime, it must be within a few minutes of their workplace. If its guests arrive by car, it must have a nearby and safe parking area. If it wishes to attract tourists, it should be near tourist attractions. Choosing a good location is perhaps the most important task in the entire process of starting a bar. Site selection is discussed in detail in Chapter 4.

GOVERNMENTAL REQUIREMENTS

Aside from money and a good location, there are important legal requirements. The liquor business is tightly regulated. Without all of the necessary licenses, permits, and approvals, you cannot open for business.

There are three levels of control for bars and taverns—federal, state, and local (city, town, and county). Federal laws apply uniformly in all 50 states and the District of Columbia, but state and local laws vary from one jurisdiction to another.

You should consult with the appropriate officials at all three levels of government early in the planning phase of your project to determine the specific requirements that apply to your situation. The appendixes of this book contain resource lists of licensing commissions and other agencies that can advise you.

FEDERAL REQUIREMENTS AND CONTROLS

The federal control agencies are the Bureau of Alcohol, Tobacco, and Firearms (BATF), the Department of Labor, and the Internal Revenue Service (IRS). Their main concerns are

- the regulation of manufacture, transportation, import, and export of alcoholic beverages;
- the adherence to federal labor laws; and
- the collection of taxes.

Special Occupational Tax Stamp

The BATF, a division of the Treasury Department, issues a *Special Occupational Tax Stamp*. Without that stamp, a proposed liquor establishment cannot legally open for business. The Special Tax Stamp is a receipt for payment of the Special Occupational Tax. It is not a federal license and does not confer any privileges on the dealer.

The law defines a retail dealer as "a person who sells alcoholic beverages to any person other than a dealer." This includes all establishments that sell alcoholic beverages for on-premise consumption, such as bars and restaurants. The Special Occupational Tax must be paid each year on or before July 1.

To pay the tax, you must obtain and file a Special Tax Registration and Return, Alcohol and Tobacco form ATF F 5630.5 (10/99). After your initial payment of this tax, you should receive a "renewal registration and return" each year prior to the due date.

The Special Tax Stamp covers only one place of business. If business is conducted at more than one location, a separate Special Tax Stamp must be obtained for each location. Persons engaged in the sale of wine, beer, or distilled spirits who willfully fail to pay the tax become liable to a fine of not more than $5,000, imprisonment for not more than two years, or both.

Any changes in location or ownership must be reported to the BATF within 30 days of their occurrence. Inspections by a BATF agent will occur periodically, therefore the Special Tax Stamp should be prominently posted or kept readily available. If your Special Tax Stamp is lost or destroyed, you should contact the BATF immediately to obtain a *Certificate in Lieu of Lost or Destroyed Special Tax Stamp*.

Records of Purchases

Another requirement of the BATF is that every retail dealer must either keep a record in book form showing the date and quantity of all distilled spirits, wine, and beer received on his or her premises and from whom received, or keep all invoices of, and bills for, all distilled spirits, wine, and beer received.

All distilled spirits bottles in a licensed beverage establishment also are required to have antitampering closures on them, of the type that when broken leave a portion of the closure on the bottle.

It is a punishable violation for a retail dealer to reuse or refill liquor bottles with distilled spirits or any substance, including water. Violations are punishable by fines of not more than $1,000, imprisonment for not more than one year, or both.

For complete details on the federal liquor laws and regulations, call the BATF office (800-937-8864) and ask for free booklet ATF P 5170.2 (Liquor Laws and Regulations for Retail Dealers).

Another government agency is the Department of Labor, which administers the provisions of the *Fair Labor Standards Act*. Its main concerns are with conformance to the federal minimum wage laws and discriminatory practices. Most employers' dealings on labor issues are conducted with state labor departments. In the event state and federal laws vary, as sometimes happens with minimum wage levels, the higher of the two minimum wage rates prevails.

The IRS requires a retail dealer of alcoholic beverages to obtain an Employer Identification Number. This is done by filing IRS form number SS-4. Aside from paying estimated federal income taxes quarterly, employers are required by the IRS to withhold federal income taxes, Social Security taxes, and Medicare taxes from their employees' pay. The withholdings must be forwarded to the IRS by the 15th day of the following month, by either making an electronic deposit directly to the IRS or by making a deposit at your commercial bank, using Federal Tax Deposit Form 8109. To calculate payroll withholdings, an employer should refer to IRS Circular E, Employer's Tax Guide. Your accountant can give you specific instruction on this.

STATE AND LOCAL REQUIREMENTS AND CONTROLS

Although the requirements for opening a bar vary from state to state, all states require a liquor license to sell alcoholic beverages at the retail level. A bar or tavern owner is a retailer. In addition, all states have regulations that govern what you can sell, where you can sell it, when and to whom you may sell it, and how you may advertise and promote it.

The type and number of licenses available also vary from state to state. The license for a bar that sells alcoholic beverages for consumption only on the licensed premises is called an *on-premise* license. There are a variety of on-premise licenses, such as restaurant, tavern, ballroom, golf course, bowling alley, and club licenses. Each type of license has special criteria that must be met. The effective term of a license is one year, and it applies to only one specific location.

All states have an Alcoholic Beverage Control (ABC) agency. In some states, only the state ABC agency issues liquor licenses. In other states, cities are allowed to issue liquor licenses, provided the state ABC agency approves the issuance of the licenses.

License States versus Control States

There are two categories of states in regards to governmental involvement in the liquor business. They are *license states* and *control states*.

In a license state, the sale of alcoholic beverages is conducted by private businesses. In these states, liquor, beer, and wine products are distributed by private wholesalers that have salespeople who call on bars. In a control state, the state is in the liquor business. In these states, bars must buy their stock from state liquor stores or warehouses. There are 18 control states and one county, and each has its own regulations.

Every state publishes a book, free or at a nominal cost, describing its liquor laws and regulations. Prospective bar owners should obtain a copy from their state ABC agency. Appendix D contains the names and telephone numbers or e-mail addresses of those agencies for all 50 states.

Liquor Licenses

In some states, new liquor licenses are difficult to obtain because they are issued on the basis of population. In other states, new licenses are readily issued as long as the applicant and the premises meet the requirements for a license. Each state has its own requirements. Applicants for liquor licenses are checked thoroughly. Of greatest concern to state liquor control boards is an applicant's ability to obey laws and be financially responsible.

Although liquor laws vary from one jurisdiction to another, they typically cover the following items:

- Types of licenses available, fees, and the application process
- Requirements for acquiring a license
- Hours and days of operation
- Proximity to churches, schools, and hospitals
- Who may be employed
- Who may not be served alcoholic beverages
- Change of ownership or managers
- Changes or alterations to the licensed premises
- Entertainment
- Adulteration of alcoholic beverages
- Advertising restrictions

The general requirements for a liquor license are:

The applicant must
• be 21 years of age or older;
• be financially responsible;
• have good moral character; and
• be an American citizen.

Before a liquor license will be issued, a bar must have a food service license, a fire permit, and, if construction or renovations are necessary, a building permit.

As with all businesses, a bar must register its name with the secretary of state and comply with the state's labor laws, handicap access regulations, and tax collection regulations. For specific details as to the requirements, you should check with the appropriate agencies in your particular state.

Food Service Licenses

The name of this license may vary from state to state (Massachusetts calls it an Innholder/Common Victualler license), but the intent is the same—to ensure that you operate in a sanitary and safe manner, meeting all the provisions of the food sanitation codes. Licenses are issued for one year at a time, and you must have one in order to operate.

State and local public health authorities cooperate closely. In some locales, local health departments administer inspections and issue food service licenses subject to approval by the state public health department. In others, state public health officials administer all aspects of the sanitation code.

The typical five-step process for obtaining a food service license is as follows:

1. Advise local officials of your proposed bar or restaurant, including:
   • Building inspector
   • Planning board
   • Zoning board

2. Submit floor plans of your establishment to the local health department, which will advise you if it is necessary to submit them to the state health department. Call to make an appointment to bring in the plans for review.
   - Show the placement of all major equipment and location of sinks and restrooms, and include a list of materials to be used for floors, walls, ceilings, and work surfaces
   - Include a copy of your proposed food and beverage menus
3. Complete and submit a license application with the appropriate fee to the local or state health department, as directed.
4. Call the health department for a preopening inspection at least seven days prior to your planned opening date.
5. A food service license or health permit will be issued, and periodic inspections will follow, if all goes well with the preopening inspection.

When planning a bar or food service facility, particular attention should be paid to toilets and hand-washing facilities, sewage disposal, plumbing, lighting, ventilation, dishwashing and glasswashing facilities, and all food contact surfaces. These are areas of vital concern to public health authorities.

Fire Permits

A bar or restaurant cannot open for business until it has been issued a fire permit. The state fire marshal's office and local fire departments work hand in hand, but as a rule, it is the local fire departments that do the on-site inspections.

The local fire department places a limit on the number of patrons allowed into an establishment. That capacity is determined by square footage and other factors contained in the state and local fire codes, which are modeled after the National Fire Protection Code.

Local fire departments issue permits upon passage of an inspection that includes, but is not limited to, the following items of concern:

- *Fire extinguishers.* There must be an adequate quantity and type with proper placement throughout the premises. They must typically be located within 75 feet from any point, have a particular rating, and be visible.

- *Exits.* There must be the proper number of exits, in the right locations, with no obstructions in the pathway, and with illuminated exit signs above them. External exit doors must swing outward and be mounted with crash bars.
- *Electrical.* All electrical work must conform to applicable building codes and be done by licensed electricians, using approved materials. There must be an adequate electrical supply to safely meet the load required by the equipment and other electrically powered systems.
- *Fire detection.* Smoke detectors and appropriate fire suppression systems (such as sprinklers, CO_2, and dry chemical dispensers) must be in place, as well as an emergency lighting system.
- *Flammable liquids.* The storage, use, and disposal of any flammable liquids (such as cooking oils) must be by approved means. Cooking equipment that utilizes combustible liquids must be protected by fire hoods with built-in suppression systems.
- *Sprinklers.* They must not be covered, blocked, or otherwise impaired from performing as intended.
- *Storage.* Aisles of at least 36" should be provided between shelves. Approved metal containers must be provided for debris or other combustible materials.
- *Clearances.* Gas-fired and other fuel-burning equipment must be installed with specified clearances from walls, ceilings, and floors.
- *Miscellaneous.* Chimneys, heating equipment, and vent systems must meet code requirements.

Building Permits

In most communities, it is necessary to check with several other agencies before scheduling the building inspection. Following is the usual sequence of events for obtaining a building permit and a certificate of occupancy:

1. Check with the zoning board to determine whether the zoning at your proposed location will allow your type of business.

2. Obtain a site approval from the planning board. This is an important step in the case of a bar, because this is when public hearings will be held and abutters may voice objection to your business. It is best to know of any objections early on.
3. A plan review meeting is held with both a building and fire department official present. They will review the plans in detail, paying particular attention to the structural integrity of the building, the occupancy capacity for which it is rated, fire detection systems, and conformance with all applicable building codes.
4. Make a formal application for a building permit.

If everything checks out well in the above stages, a building permit is issued and construction may be started. From this point on, the building inspector will make periodic inspections of the construction to determine compliance with codes. You must use licensed electricians and plumbers.

When the construction is completed, the building inspector and the health inspector will make a final inspection. Upon passage of those inspections, a certificate of occupancy is issued to the owner of the business.

Other State or Local Departments

You also may need to contact the following state and local departments:

- *Secretary of State*. Here you register the name of the business, and incorporate, if that is the legal form of business chosen.
- *Commission on the Handicapped*. This is where you can inquire about accessibility requirements for new construction and renovations.
- *Bureau of Weights and Measures*. They conduct inspection of any scales to be used for commercial trade.
- *Department of Revenue*. This is where you get information on sales taxes or meals taxes that may have to be collected.
- *Signage Commission*. Many communities now have an agency that controls signage and requires that a permit be obtained before a sign may be installed. They are primarily concerned with the size

(square footage) of the sign, its height from ground level, and the type of illumination planned for it.

- *Historical Commission.* If you plan to utilize a designated historical building for your business, you may not be able to do the things you want with it. Similarly, if you wish to establish a business within a historical district, you will have strict restrictions on what you may or may not do to the property.
- *Wetlands Commission.* If you are looking at a property for your business that contains wetlands, you may not be able to fill it in for your parking lot. Inquire first.

In recent years, water supply and septic systems have come under much tighter control, as has the disposal of hazardous materials. These are important matters to investigate when buying a property, particularly in suburban areas where wells and septic systems are common. Beware, as well, of underground fuel tanks that may have to be removed at considerable cost.

Actio n **G**u i d e l i n e s

✓ Obtain specific information on the requirements for opening a bar in your location by doing the following:

  a. Contact your local regulatory agencies:
- Liquor commission
- Public health department
- Planning board

  b. Contact your state regulatory agencies:
- Alcoholic Beverage Control agency
- State Public Health Department
- State Labor Department
- State Department of Finance and Taxation

  c. Contact the Bureau of Alcohol, Tax, and Firearms

  d. Contact the Internal Revenue Service

✓ Consult an accountant and an attorney familiar with the requirements for obtaining licenses and opening bars.

✓ Estimate the approximate cost of starting the type of bar you have
in mind, and match it with your possible sources of funds, using the
resources described in this chapter.

4

PREPARING FOR SUCCESS

Now that you have decided you are suited for the business and have determined that you can meet the requirements for starting a bar, the next step is to conduct a feasibility study to determine your prospects for success. This will require interacting with the community you choose to learn what its socioeconomic conditions are. Ask yourself the following questions: What is the outlook for its business sector? In that environment, will your project, as you envision it, succeed? Can it be located properly? Is what you are planning wanted or needed? What is the level of competition to be encountered? The answers to these and other questions will indicate the feasibility of proceeding with the project.

WHY SO MANY NEW BUSINESSES FAIL

The ingredients for entrepreneurial success have been studied for a long time, but to date no one has come up with a formula that works in every case. The best you can hope for is that with diligence, training, experience, good planning, and responsible execution of your plans, you stand a chance of succeeding. And, you can increase your chances by learning from the experience of others.

Some people think owning a bar is a sure way to riches. Others believe bars can endure the worst of economic times and even survive poor management, because alcoholic beverages have such a high markup. The facts show, however, that many bars fail each year.

Eighty percent of all new businesses fail within the first five years of their existence, and bars are no exception. As with most unsuccessful businesses, two main causes of failure stand out: One is undercapitalization, and the other is lack of knowledge about the business.

Undercapitalization, which simply put means "not having enough money to do the job," usually results from not having a financial plan when entering business. Some entrepreneurs use all of their funds to buy a business and do not have enough money left to meet the first month's bills. Some overspend on new equipment or renovations rather than phase in changes on a schedule that would match their cash flow. In the event a prospective buyer or builder does not have enough capital to enter the business safely, it is best to hold off until the capital position is improved.

Lack of knowledge of the business covers a broad spectrum from not knowing one's guests to not having the necessary training or experience in the field. Money alone cannot buy profitability. Some investors who have adequate funds to enter a business, but lack the interest or ability to manage it properly, unfortunately wind up with losses instead of profits. Proprietors must constantly monitor their business and look for weak spots that need improvement.

The following recommendations will help you stay in business:

- Create a sound business plan before buying or starting a business.
- Seek guidance from a reputable accountant and lawyer, preferably acquainted with the hospitality field.
- Broaden your knowledge of the business as much as possible through personal research, reading trade journals and books, talking with salespeople, attending professional seminars, and taking useful courses.
- Join your local professional associations and network with other restaurant and bar owners.
- Utilize your suppliers as educational resources on new products, trends, and promotional ideas.
- Develop a financial plan (cash flow, budget) for your first year in business.

- Compare your actual performance against your plan at frequent intervals during the year.
- Control the following profit centers carefully from the outset of your business:
  - *Purchasing.* Establish specifications for each product (purveyor, brand, bottle size, maximum and minimum stock levels).
  - *Receiving.* Count and inspect all incoming shipments for proper quantity and breakage before signing invoices.
  - *Storing.* Put away all incoming shipments of liquor, beer, and wine immediately, and keep them in locked storage. Issue a minimum of keys to the liquor storeroom—and only to supervisory or management personnel.
  - *Issuing.* Record all additions to issues from inventory in an inventory book.
  - *Inventory.* Take a physical inventory (actually counted) weekly, preferably, but at least once a month to verify the accuracy of the balances on-hand shown in the inventory book.
  - *Drink mixing and serving.* Use standard recipes and standard glass sizes for all drinks.
  - *Cashiering.* Make sure every drink is accounted for, according to your policies. If you want to give away a drink, fine, it is your business. But no one else should have the right to give away your profits.
- Know your guests. The better you know them individually and as a class, the better you will be able to serve them. Some ways of categorizing your guests are age, sex, income, interests, type of jobs, education levels, type of transportation, and brand preferences.
- Observe your guests' spending habits. Where are they spending their money? What are they buying? How much do they tend to spend? What time do they arrive? How long do they stay? Do they come alone or with friends?
- Establish and adhere to responsible business practices. This will affect your relations with your liquor control board and your acceptance by the community.
- Keep up-to-date on liquor laws and regulations.
- Advertise effectively to attract the type of clientele you desire.
- Make your guests feel welcome; talk to them and get feedback.

- Give your guests reasons to come back again soon. Develop a steady flow of promotional events and announce them on table tents and wall posters.
- Price your drinks competitively, according to your particular style of service.
- Serve high-quality drinks.
- Keep your premises clean and updated.

Finally, management should conduct periodic surveys of the business to identify problems and anticipate possible causes of failure. Corrective action should be taken as soon as possible. Assess corrective actions soon after implementation to determine their effectiveness and to detect any unforeseen adverse consequences of an action.

For example, suppose the ABC Lounge is losing guests to the XYZ Lounge, a new competitor that has entertainment. In response, ABC begins to offer entertainment. After two weeks, ABC reviews the situation and finds sales are still declining and, on top of that, profits have shrunk because of the cost of the entertainment. The corrective action must be assessed. Possibly, they have engaged the wrong type of entertainment for their clientele. Or, it may be that the competitor's entertainment is not what is drawing the guests away. It might be that the quality of food or drinks at the ABC Lounge has slipped or any number of other reasons. The point is, ABC must recognize that the corrective action has not achieved the desired result and modify it.

Management must be honest and objective in its appraisal of how good the business is performing. Be your severest critic, because no one else cares as much as you do about the success of your business.

TWO APPROACHES TO ENTERING THE BUSINESS

As with most other small businesses, there are two approaches to entry: start a new bar or tavern, or buy an existing one. Neither approach is a surefire guarantee of success. However, having knowledge of the factors involved in each can significantly improve your chances of succeeding.

Should You Start a New Business?

If you have a truly unique concept and have (or can raise) the necessary funding, you will probably want to launch your bar as a new business. If extensive renovations are required, they can eradicate most of the savings associated with buying an existing business and oftentimes do not render the desired result.

In starting a new business, you are pioneering your concept. Everything you do will have already been done in an established business. The difference is you will be able to do it your way. However, you will have to address all of the responsibilities of a business start-up. For example, you will have to establish an organization, find a suitable location, develop your menu and liquor list, determine prices, project sales, purchase equipment, select your décor, develop a service system, plan your entertainment format, and hire and train a new staff.

When all of these things are done, you will open your doors to the public and hope your new business will be a success. You can never be sure until the operation is tested in the marketplace, toe to toe against the competition.

Figure 4.1 depicts the typical progression of activities associated with starting up a bar business when adequate financing is in place. If external financing is required, you will have to plan the project up to the point of estimating its cost and potential return before approaching investors or lenders. The cost of the project must be reasonable in terms of its potential return. If the estimated costs are excessive, you will have to loop back in the process and make the changes necessary to complete the project with available funds. Consultants, experienced in the hospitality field, may be engaged to assist with equipment selection and costing. The talents, financial resources, and experience of the principals make every start-up situation unique; however, the basic process tends to be the same.

Should You Buy an Existing Business?

If you buy an existing business, you will have a going concern with an immediate cash flow, and you will save the start-up costs of a new business. Care must be taken to ensure you do not inherit unwanted problems, such as an irreparable bad reputation, an incompetent staff,

FIGURE 4.1 *Flow Chart of Activities for a Start-up Bar Business*

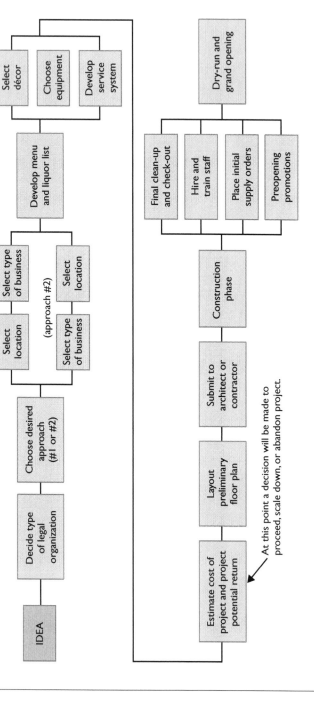

outdated equipment, or a short lease. Arrange to have an equipment specialist accompany you when you inspect the business. Look at the age and condition of the equipment, and determine if it was cleaned well and cared for properly. Obtain assurance from the Alcoholic Beverage Commission that the liquor license may be transferred to you.

HOW MUCH SHOULD YOU PAY?

The answer to this question will vary with the facts of each situation. There is no one rule of thumb. For instance, if you were considering buying a business in its entirety—a going operation with a successful track record and cash flow—it would be valued one way; whereas, if you intend to buy just the assets of a business, they would be valued quite differently. In the first case, the price would be based on the value of the assets plus the value of a proven income stream. In the second case, the price would be based solely on the value of the assets, which unless utilized properly, may or may not produce profits.

Similarly, if a business were located in an extraordinarily good location, it would command a substantial premium over the price of one in a mediocre location.

Potential buyers may use several techniques to assess an existing business and use the results to determine a high and low end of an acceptable price range. This is an area where you should work closely with your accountant. Here are four of the more common methods:

1. *Comparable values of similar going concerns.* This method arrives at a value based on what similar businesses have sold for.
2. *Reproduction or replacement value.* This method is based on the open-market cost of reproducing the assets of the business. It is most useful when only the assets of a business are being purchased.
3. *Earnings approach.* This method focuses on the annual earnings of the business. Earnings can be used to calculate your potential return on investment; however, some cautions are important.

    For example, earnings can vary with methods of accounting. In the case of a sole proprietorship, if the owner worked but did not take a salary, the business's earnings would appear much higher than they otherwise would be. Also, if economic conditions have shifted and are now declining, past performance may not be a good indicator of what can be expected in the future.

Some people will use a multiple of annual earnings to establish a theoretical value that fits their amortization timetable. However, in the end you must regard earnings as only one measure that must be looked at alongside the others.

4. *Book value.* Essentially this is the adjusted book value of a business, arrived at by subtracting total liabilities from total assets and adjusting for any intangibles, such as goodwill. Although the data is based on a firm's most recent balance sheet, the value of the assets should be tested for fair market value and, if necessary, so restated.

WHAT SHOULD YOU PAY FOR RENT?

The words location, location, location dictate the value of rents. Time and place are all important. Time refers to what is happening at a location within a given period. For instance, a storefront one block away from an Olympic Village during an Olympic year will fetch a far greater rent than it would at another time. Similarly, a storefront located between two popular anchor stores in a high-volume mall would garner a higher rent than a store in a less desirable location.

Rent is also influenced by factors other than the traffic count. The age of a building and the prestige value of its address, as well as the provision of amenities, such as heat, light, water, parking, and snow removal, will affect rents. When expenses, such as property taxes, insurance, and maintenance, are paid by the lessee, the lease is referred to as a triple net lease. A National Restaurant Association publication, *Restaurant Industry Operations Report 2004,* shows occupancy costs (which include rent, property taxes, and insurance) for full-menu, table service restaurants that sell both food and beverages range from 3 percent to 10 percent of total sales depending on the quality of the location.

It is important when planning to be conservative in estimating total sales so as to not elevate expenses that are forecast as a percentage of sales.

EVALUATING AN OPPORTUNITY

It is vital that you research a business carefully before buying it. Figure 4.2 presents a checklist for surveying an existing beverage establishment. It also can be used as a guide or reference list at many stages of the planning process. It will remind you of things that might easily be overlooked.

Professional Assistance

In addition to a checklist, use experts to help you evaluate the business. Talk to bankers, suppliers, and repairmen. They can give you information about many aspects of the business. Also talk to patrons, neighbors, and anyone else who may have information about the business. Try to find out how the business has been doing in regard to sales, public image, and guest satisfaction. Most of all, be sure to get your accountant and lawyer involved at this stage of your evaluation.

Insist that your accountant be permitted to examine the official books of the business. Check on outstanding bills and tax obligations if you buy the business in its entirety. If deposits for future business (functions booked in advance) have been accepted by the current owner, adjustments should be made during the closing process. The tax status of the business should be examined carefully. Have all taxes been paid or are there tax issues to be resolved with the IRS?

CLOSING THE DEAL

Engage a lawyer who is familiar with the hospitality industry. If you need a referral, contact your local bar association, which can give you several names. Your lawyer should be present at all signings and should review all documents before you sign them. You will be encountering contractual matters that are beyond the ability of the average layperson to cope with. Make any agreements contingent upon your acquiring the necessary licenses and permits, because without your licenses and permits you will not be able to open for business.

FIGURE 4.2   *Checklist for Surveying an Existing Beverage Establishment*

Areas to Evaluate	Comments
1. Beverage purchasing and receiving procedures	
2. Beverage storing and issuing methods	
3. Bar equipment and layout	
a. Location of equipment	
b. Maintenance of equipment	
c. Efficient placement	
4. Functional aspects of beverage dispensing equipment	
a. Cleanability	
b. Attractive design	
c. Ease of operation	
5. Drink preparation methods	
a. Quality control—recipes	
b. Use of premixes	
c. Portion control	
d. Showmanship	
6. Inventory selections	
a. Item popularity	
b. Product availability	
c. Price range	
7. Personnel	
a. Staffing	
b. Duties and responsibilities	
c. Grooming	
d. Uniforms	
e. Productivity	
f. Morale	
8. Labor	
a. Turnover of employees	
b. Training on the job	
c. Overtime policies	

FIGURE 4.2   *Checklist for Surveying an Existing Beverage Establishment (Continued)*

Areas to Evaluate	Comments
9. Bar costs	
a. Standard drink recipes	
b. Inventory control records	
c. Pilferage control	
d. Calculation of bar cost percentages	
10. Drink presentation methods	
a. Size of drinks	
b. Garnishing the drinks	
c. Cashiering the system	
11. Service system	
a. Drink ordering	
b. Pick-up system	
c. Guest check controls	
d. Drink delivery system	
12. Lounge	
a. Number of cocktail servers	
b. Tables per station	
c. Style of service	
d. Décor	
e. Type of clientele	
f. Average guest check size	
13. China, glassware, utensils, paper supplies	
a. Backup inventory supply	
b. Inventory-taking procedures	
c. Reorder policies	
14. Advertising, sales, promotion	
a. Types of ads, frequency	
b. Media used	
c. Method for developing ads	

FIGURE 4.2 *Checklist for Surveying an Existing Beverage Establishment (Continued)*

Areas to Evaluate	Comments
15. Sanitation	
a. Policies	
b. Training	
c. Equipment	
d. Method of supervision	
16. Safety	
a. Fire extinguishing equipment	
b. Fire exits	
c. Fire retardant materials	
d. Emergency lighting	
17. Communications	
a. Lines of authority	
b. Supervision	
c. Policy manual	
18. Accounting controls	
a. Food cost controls	
b. Beverage cost controls	
c. Labor cost controls	
19. Physical appearance of property	
a. Building	
b. Furniture, fixtures, and equipment	
c. Obsolescence factor	

SELECTING YOUR LEGAL FORM OF BUSINESS

There are a number of legal forms of business from which you may choose: the sole proprietorship, the partnership (general and limited), the corporation, the S corporation, and the limited liability corporation (LLC). Each has its advantages and disadvantages. At issue will be how much money you have to invest, how much personal involvement in the business you wish to undertake, tax implications, liability disclosure requirements, and your growth plans. Which legal form of business is best for you is a matter that should be worked out with your lawyer and accountant.

Sole Proprietorship

The sole proprietorship is popular because it gives the owner complete domination over a business. The owner can make the rules and set the policies, take time off at will or work long hours. Best of all, the owner gets to keep all of the after-tax profits, and the profits are taxed as personal income. The idea of no boss or committee meetings is very appealing. In addition, the owner enjoys prestige, hires and fires people, and has final authority for everything.

The other side of the sole proprietorship picture is that the owner must carry the entire financial burden of the business and be competent at all of the roles he or she assumes. The greatest disadvantage of a sole proprietorship is its unlimited liability. The personal assets of the proprietor are at risk if the business fails or is sued.

Partnership

Small partnerships enjoy some of the advantages of a sole proprietorship except that everything you own, do, or earn is shared with one or more partners. There are two basic types of partnerships: *general* and *limited*.

In a *general partnership,* all partners have unlimited liability. In a *limited partnership,* there must be at least one general partner who runs the business and has unlimited liability and an unrestricted number of limited partners who have limited liability and are not required to take an active role in the operations of the business.

Partnerships function best when the partners have complementary talents and each brings financial resources to the business. A partnership agreement should be drawn up by an attorney and signed by all partners. At the very least, it should include the names of all partners, the amount of each partner's investment, the share of the firm's profits to which each partner will be entitled, the role and responsibilities of each partner in the operations of the business, and what will happen in the event a partner dies or wants to sell his or her ownership share.

Be very careful about the individuals with whom you become a partner. One partner's actions may jeopardize a business and create a liability that must be shared by all partners. Unless you need the skills or the funds of others to launch your business, you have no reason to consider the partnership form of business.

Corporation

The Supreme Court defines a corporation as "a fictitious person." Consequently, because you are a real person, you cannot be a corporation. A corporation is a separate entity from yourself. You can, however, be a stockholder, a director, an officer, or an employee of a corporation. Three or more persons can obtain a corporate charter and elect a board of directors, which directs the corporation, and appoint officers to run it. Following is a list of advantages of incorporating:

- Your liability is limited to your investment in the corporation (unless you misuse corporate funds or facilities).
- Your personal assets are protected from seizure or attachment by corporate creditors or lawsuits.
- Filing a Sub-Chapter S election allows gains and losses to flow directly through to stockholders, so that they can be treated as personal income. (In this respect, the Sub-Chapter S corporation is treated like a partnership.) Certain IRS requirements must be met to qualify for this election.
- An LLC, in states where allowed, is an alternative to partnerships and corporations. It combines the corporate advantage of limited liability with the partnership advantage of pass-through taxation. This form of organization is popular with smaller companies that have limited growth plans.
- Raising additional capital for growth or expansion is easier than with a proprietorship or partnership.
- Stock can be used as collateral for loans, whereas proprietorships and partnerships may have to use their personal assets.

RAISING ADDITIONAL CAPITAL

This is where the corporate form of business has a distinct advantage over other forms. A corporation may sell additional shares of stock without affecting the workings of the company because its owners are legally separated from the operations of the company. A corporation can also obtain debt capital from professional lending institutions.

A sole proprietor cannot sell stock and must borrow additional capital on the strength of his or her personal and business reputation. If you are an established member of your business community with an upstanding reputation and are well networked in local financial circles, borrowing as a private individual should not present a problem. However, if you are new to a community, you will find it more difficult.

Partnerships have the ability to bring new partners with investment capital into the firm. However, finding the right persons with whom to associate is not always an easy matter. Extreme caution must be exercised because of the unlimited liability feature of a general partnership.

SELECTING A LOCATION AND PROPERTY

The checklist in Figure 4.3 can be useful when examining sites. It is a good idea to use a recording device to store information as you evaluate potential sites. Not all items in the checklist are applicable in every situation.

SELECTING A NAME

The actual process of registering a business name is an easy matter. Simply obtain the appropriate forms from the secretary of state's office (in your state capital), fill them out specifying your desired names, and return them to the secretary of state with a check for the stipulated fee. It is wise to submit three desired names in their order of preference. The names will be screened through a computer, and if no one else has already registered the name you want, you will get it. That is the legal side of selecting a name.

FIGURE 4.3 *Site Analysis Checklist*

Address of Site:	Present Owner or Agent:
City/State/Zip: _____	Address:_____
Lot No.:_____	City/State/Zip: _____
Map Ref.: _____	Tel.: _____
Date of Inspection: _____	Asking Price: _____

Physical Features of the Land

Size:	Approach/visibility:
Shape:	Accessibility to target:
Slope:	Clearance:
Expansion possibilities:	Zoning:
Utilities:	Nearby hazards or blights:
Water, gas, electricity, sewers	Parking possibilities:
Soil conditions:	Snow removal or storage space:
perc tests, drainage	

Economic and Community Features

Economic trend:	Wage trends:
Public transportation:	Competition:
Local attractions:	Income levels:
Civic promotional/agencies:	Seasonal features:
Labor supply:	Major highways nearby:
Population (number and makeup):	Fire and police protection:
Daily traffic:	Food and beverage suppliers:
Auto count:	
Pedestrian count:	

Physical Features of the Structure

This is a partial list. Your real estate agent can supply you with additional information.

Perimeter dimensions:	Type of siding and roofing:
No. of rooms and sizes:	Electrical service (amps, phase):
Traffic flow lines:	Gas service (LP or natural, size):
No. of restrooms:	Sewer (municipal or septic tank):
Flooring materials:	Water (munic. or well, volume):

FIGURE 4.3 *Site Analysis Checklist (Continued)*

Storage possibilities:	Handicap accessibility:
Insulation:	Heating/ventilation/AC:
Laws and Restrictions	
Zoning of property:	Building height and set-back:
Land-use and environmental laws:	Requirement:
Permits and licenses needed:	Lighting and signage:
Building restrictions:	Other requirements:
Wetland restrictions:	
Taxes	
Property tax:	Meals and lodging tax:
Income or business tax:	State sales tax:
Assessment percentage:	Water and sewer tax:
City sales tax:	
Cost of Property	
Land:	Necessary improvements:
Building:	Total investment:
Data may be obtained from tax offices, registry of deeds books, town or city clerks, real estate agents and brokers, highway departments, chambers of commerce, as well as on-site inspections.	

The public relations side is equally important. Thoughtful consideration should be given to your name because it can serve many purposes. Here are some examples of names and their functions:

- The Dockside Lounge—suggests a nautical atmosphere
- The Alameda Cantina—implies Mexican food
- The Bridge Street Café—tells you where it is located
- The Music Box Lounge—tells you they feature music
- The Old Sod Pub—indicates an Irish pub

If you plan to have a Web site for promotional purposes, you should check out the names that you are considering on a Web browser such as Google to determine if the Web address that you would like is still available. This might affect your choice of names.

Think about the message you want your name to convey in terms of your target market and its wants and expectations.

MANAGING RISK

Acquiring adequate insurance, training your staff, and setting sound company policies are the three main ways to manage risk. A successful risk management program must incorporate all three. It is advisable to have an insurance agent or broker design a complete insurance program for your business. Types of insurance available include the following:

- *Liquor liability*. Protects against suits resulting from damages or injuries to others by a person who became intoxicated in your establishment
- *Property damage*. Covers buildings, inventory, equipment, and fixtures against loss due to fire, smoke, explosion, or vandalism
- *General comprehensive liability*. Covers claims for bodily injury and property damage due to an accident
- *Personal injury liability*. Covers lawsuits due to false arrest, libel, slander, defamation of character, and personal injuries
- *Automobile liability*. Covers damages or injuries that employees incur while driving their car or a company car in the performance of company business
- *Product liability*. Covers against lawsuits based on damages or injuries resulting from a product that you served
- *Fire*. Covers damages to other buildings from a fire that originated on your property
- *Workers' compensation*. Covers employees' medical and rehabilitation costs for work-related injuries
- *Business interruption*. Reimburses you for expenses incurred and for revenues and profits lost as a result of unintended interruption of your business due to fire, major theft, or illness of a key employee
- *Bonds*. Covers against lawsuits for financial loss incurred by others due to an act or default of an employee or to some contingency over which the principal may have no control

Some carriers specialize in insuring beverage establishments. Their rates will vary according to the type of business, condition of the premises, degree of exposure to risks, and your risk management program.

Action **G**uidelines

✓ Evaluate the relative merits of buying a going bar business as opposed to starting one.

✓ Acquaint yourself with lawyers and accountants who have experience in the hospitality industry and use them for guidance.

✓ Select a legal form of business for your business.

✓ Choose three names for your bar.

✓ Work with an insurance broker to develop a risk management program to meet the needs of your business.

5

PLANNING FOR PROFITS

THE MAIN BUILDING BLOCK OF A START-UP IS THE BUSINESS PLAN

A business plan is a blueprint of how you will operate your proposed business. It is also a communications instrument that tells others the course of action by which you intend to achieve your goals. A start-up business without a sound business plan is like a ship without a rudder, floating aimlessly amid external forces that may doom it.

A business plan can serve a number of purposes, including persuading someone to support your project financially. However, its first and foremost value is to focus your thinking on what you wish to achieve and how you intend to do it. Preparing a business plan forces you to think through every aspect of your prospective business. If there are weaknesses, they will become evident as you work through the plan. Beyond that, your business plan can serve as a road map through your start-up period and be a reference point against which you can periodically compare your actual results.

When preparing your business plan, it is essential that you be sure of your facts and be prepared to defend their validity. Investors and lenders will consider false or incomplete information as unreliable or deceptive. Apart from that, inaccurate information will mislead you in evaluating your project's chances for success.

A well-written business plan will convey to its readers the impression that you can think clearly and have the ability to successfully run a business.

ESTIMATING YOUR START-UP COSTS

There are numerous sources for information on costs. Equipment suppliers will provide you with working figures on bar and food service equipment. Commercial real estate agents can supply cost data and advice on suitable properties. Architects and contractors, interested in your business, will give you ballpark figures as you consider the feasibility of your project. Distributors of food, liquor, beer, and wine can assist you in estimating inventory costs. Because you are a potential client, it is in their best interest to help you with your early planning. Whenever possible, cross-check information with more than one source.

If your business is a sole proprietorship or partnership, you will have limited capital. Consequently, the matter of estimating start-up costs will happen in stages, starting with ballpark figures. As your ideas become better defined, your estimates will become more realistic. At each stage of the process, you must answer the question, "Can I afford it?" If you believe you can, then you will proceed to obtain final figures, and that might entail hiring a consultant to develop a reliable estimate for you.

If you do not feel you can afford the project, based on the ballpark figures, you must go back to square one and scale down your ideas or abandon the project.

If your business is a corporation, you will have the opportunity to raise unlimited funds through the sale of stock. However, your potential investors will scrutinize your business plan carefully and will want to be convinced of the business's chances of success and the anticipated rate of return on investment.

The format for business plans can vary, but certain sections of information commonly appear in all business plans. An outline of a typical business plan is shown in Figure 5.1, and is followed by detailed explanations of the type of information that might appear in each section. A complete sample business plan for a bar and grill appears in Appendix A.

FIGURE 5.1   *Outline of a Business Plan*

Cover Page
Table of Contents
Statement of Purpose

Part One: The Business
- Description of the Business
- Background of the Business
- The Company's Mission Statement
- The Concept
- Location
- Industry Trends
- Other Resources
- The Management
- Objectives and Financial Expectations
- Product and Service
- Pricing and Profitability
- Product Life Cycle
- Market Analysis
- Competition
- Guests
- Marketing Strategy
- Personnel
- Risk
- Loan Request and Anticipated Benefits
- Summary of Part One

Part Two: Financial Projections
- Start-up Requirements
- Estimated Annual Sales
- List of Furniture, Fixtures, and Equipment
- Leasehold Improvements
- Sources and Uses of Funds
- Income Statement for First Year
- Projected Income Statement—Month by Month
- Cash Flow Statement by Month
- Daily Break-even Analysis
- Conclusion and Summary of Part Two

Part Three: Supporting Documents
Supporting documents include all legal and professional documents that
support the information contained in Parts One and Two. In addition, the
following should be included: personal résumés of all principals, personal
balance sheets, credit reports, letters of recommendation, letters of intent,
copies of leases and contracts, and any other applicable documents that will
strengthen the plan.

DESCRIPTION OF A BUSINESS PLAN

The Cover Page

The cover page tells the reader who you are. It should include

- the name of your company;
- the date the business plan is issued;
- the name and title of the principal person submitting the plan;
- the address and telephone number of the business; and
- the number of the plan (if you are submitting multiple copies of the plan).

Table of Contents

The table of contents lists what is contained and where it appears in your business plan. The page numbers should not be inserted until after the plan is completed in every other respect.

You should number the pages using chapter and page numbers, such as 1.1, 1.2, 1.3 for Chapter 1; 2.1, 2.2, 2.3 for Chapter 2; and so on. This allows you to add pages at the end of each chapter at the last minute without having to renumber the entire document. For clarity, always start new sections on a new page. Business plans will typically run 20 or more pages.

Statement of Purpose

Explain, in a summarized way, what the rest of the report will cover in detail. Answer the who, what, when, where, and how questions:

- Who is the report about? Who is asking for the loan?
- What is the business? What is your legal form of ownership (sole proprietorship, partnership, corporation, Sub-Chapter S corporation)?
- How much funding is sought?

- What will the funds be used for?
- What benefits will result to the business from the use of the funds?
- How will the borrowed funds be repaid? If you are seeking outside funding, this information will be of great interest to the lender. If you are preparing the business plan for your own use, it should be of equal interest for you to know the business's prospects for achieving your desired profit objective.

Part One: The Business

In this section, you will describe the business and tell what it will do, and how it will do it.

Description of the company. Provide your business's name and intended starting date. State the products and services, days and hours of business, and the names of the investors and their roles in the business.

Background of the business. Describe the idea and your research findings from surveys and interviews. Indicate why the findings support your proposed business.

Company's mission statement. This is a statement of your overall goal for the company, throughout its lifetime, as you now see it.

Concept. Describe the concept in detail and explain its unique-ness. Tell how your business will fit into the marketplace and focus on the desirability of your concept. Photographs and illustrations are useful in highlighting key items of interest. Lengthy exhibits should be placed in the appendix at the back of the business plan and referenced in the body of the text.

Location. Indicate why you have chosen the proposed site and de-scribe its features. Use your Property Analysis Checklist to obtain this in-formation.

Industry trends. Describe what industry analysts predict for the next year or two. Reference the sources from which the information was obtained, such as the National Restaurant Association, your state hospitality association, the Licensed Beverage Industry Association, the Bureau of Alcohol, Tobacco & Firearms, trade journals, census data, and the like.

Other resources. For financial resources, list your food and equipment suppliers and state their credit terms. Also, list professional resources, such as your lawyer, accountant, banker, insurance agent, and/ or consultant.

Management. Describe your management team. Cover the personal histories of the owners and top employees. State their training and experience, and point out how they are suited to the duties and responsibilities they will be assuming. Their proposed salaries should be stipulated as well as anything about them that will enhance the business's chances for success.

Objectives and financial expectations. Enumerate your short-term and long-term goals for sales, guest acceptance, growth, and expansion. Tell where you want the business to go. Relate what you wish to achieve. Stress quality, profits, return on investment, and public service. Your objectives should be feasible, understandable, and realistic in terms of your resources.

Describe the benefits that investors and lenders may expect to realize when the business's near- and long-term objectives are met. The point here is to convince potential investors or lenders that all aspects of the project have been carefully considered and that the idea makes sense. Be accurate and thorough.

Product and service. Differentiate your product and service from that of your competitors; describe its benefits. Here is where you inform the reader how the business will fill a market niche and meet the needs of your target market. Stress your competitive advantages. If your concept or product is based on any proprietary secrets, such as recipes, you will want to protect them by asking investors and lenders to sign a nondisclosure agreement.

Pricing and profitability. Explain your pricing strategy and its profit-generating potential. Relate your prices to costs as well as to your competitors' strategies. Use the profit potential to estimate the payback period for investors and lenders. Copies of price lists should be included in the appendix.

Product life cycle. Describe the expected life cycle for your concept or product in the targeted marketing area. If your concept is one that has a high front-end acceptance (such as trendy dance clubs), but has a limited life expectancy, point out the quick payback and high earnings potential.

Market analysis. Define your market clearly and include charts where applicable. This section describes the market situation as it currently exists and must leave no doubt in the investors' or lenders' minds that the proposed business is appropriate for the market.

Discuss any economic conditions or market changes that may be taking place. Tell how they will benefit the business. Indicate the size of the marketing area and its potential for future growth. Detail your strengths and emphasize your marketing plans as much as your product. Point out any unexploited opportunities you recognize.

You should be realistic and identify any weaknesses you or the business may have, because the business plan is for your edification as well. Describe the ways you plan to eliminate or improve on the weaknesses. This may be the first test of how well suited you are for the business.

Competition. Identify your five or six nearest competitors. Elucidate the process by which you obtained information about your competitors to give your findings credibility. Tell what they offer and how they advertise (frequency, type of media used, and size of advertisements), and show how that compares with your plans. Indicate the competition's strengths and weaknesses and explain how your marketing strategy addresses them.

Guests. Detail the demographics of your targeted clientele—who they are, where they live, their level of education, their income bracket, their spending habits, and their wants and needs as evidenced by research. Describe their motivation to patronize your establishment. What benefits will they receive? Why can you expect they will be attracted to your business?

Marketing strategy. This part of your business plan will guide you as you respond to business conditions and opportunities. It can make the difference between mediocrity and the achievement of your goals. Your marketing strategy tells how you intend to position your business in the guest's mind and how, by contrast, you can reposition your competitors'.

Detail the segment of the market you are targeting to reach and the market share you expect to capture. Describe the selling and advertising tactics you will use to accomplish your goals. List the outside resources—public relations agencies, ad agencies, media—and the sales promotional campaigns you intend to utilize, and who will be responsible for these areas.

Personnel. Describe your hours and days of business, and your style of service. These factors will reflect how many of each type of employee you will need, and the skills required. An organization chart accompanied by a proposed personnel schedule could be included here, along with estimated payroll costs.

Risk. Show that you understand the risks of the business and have plans for managing them. These might include specialized training for employees, insurance programs, and cost controls.

Loan request and anticipated benefits. This section is used when seeking external funding and should state the sum being applied for, an itemized list of the intended uses of the funds, and the benefits that will be realized from their utilization. The display of sources and uses of funds will be restated in the Financial Projections section of Part Two.

Summary of Part One

The summary consists of a few paragraphs that capsulize the contents of Part One. They should tell who you are, what you want to do, how you plan to do it, when and where, what it will cost, why it is feasible, what the benefits are, and, where applicable, how much you want to borrow.

Financial Projections and Supporting Documents

The financial statements that compose Part Two of the business plan will be discussed in greater detail in Chapter 10.

The supporting documents section may include market survey data, drawings, and layouts; all legal and professional documents that support the information contained in Parts One and Two; as well as credit reports, letters of recommendation, letters of intent, and copies of leases, contracts, and any other documents that will strengthen the plan.

A *ction* **G** *uidelines*

✓ Firm up the concept of your proposed business venture and be able to describe it clearly.

✓ Talk to business brokers and real estate agents to determine business conditions in the market areas in which you are interested.

✓ Conduct market research; study your target market; and know the wants and needs of your prospective clientele.

✓ Evaluate the opportunities and the competition.

✓ Use the outline of a business plan in Appendix A as a guide for writing your own business plan.

✓ Determine your financial needs.

✓ Present the business plan to prospective investors or lenders (if applicable), or use it for your own purposes.

C h a p t e r

6

FACILITIES AND
EQUIPMENT PLANNING

The decisions you make at the out-
set of your project will determine the joys or problems you may experience for years to come. For that reason, careful consideration should be
given up front to the products you will be offering—drinks, food, entertainment, music, dancing, unique style of service, etc. Everything that
you offer must be scrutinized, because it is those things that will dictate
the physical layout, as well as the equipment, of an establishment. Every
decision made should be focused on delivering the best possible product
to your targeted clientele.

Consider your atmosphere, as well: Do you want to be perceived as a
high-energy bar with lots of activity and loud music, or as a conversa-
tional lounge with comfortable seating and soft background music?
Once you understand your target clientele's wants and needs and have
clearly defined your product, you are ready to design your facility.

DETERMINING YOUR EQUIPMENT NEEDS

There are several ways to determine your equipment needs. One is
to hire an architect who specializes in restaurants and bars to plan, design, and build your facility. The architect will engage subcontractors to

design each of the specialized areas of the project, a common practice for large jobs.

If yours is a small, uncomplicated project, such as adding a bar in an existing room in your restaurant, you can act as your own contractor. Fortunately, equipment vendors are very willing to help businesses calculate their needs and lay out a facility. They have the required expertise and are acquainted with the latest products on the market. You can benefit from the experience they bring from other projects. If your funds are tight, they also can help you work within budget by suggesting alternatives.

In order for vendors to work successfully with you, however, they must have exact data regarding the size and shape of the rooms involved, the seating capacity, and your products and services.

SHOULD YOU BUY OR LEASE EQUIPMENT?

On occasion a business will have the opportunity to lease a particular piece of equipment. There are valid reasons for leasing and for buying equipment, but they vary from business to business and from time to time. Consequently, there is not a single answer on deciding between leasing and buying. It is important to understand the advantages and disadvantages of each course of action, as shown in Figure 6.1.

Perhaps the most important realization when considering leasing is that "nothing is free." Everything you buy or lease has a price that includes all expenses, plus a profit for the supplier. The main reason many people lease equipment is they just don't have the money to buy it.

Another reason for at least considering leasing is as a hedge when a new business is uncertain of its future. Assuming a short-term lease, the lessee can terminate business with minimal losses as opposed to a business that buys everything and gets stuck with a lot of money tied up in used equipment. It should be noted that used food and beverage equipment is plentiful and brings very little money at auction.

LAYING OUT AN EFFICIENT FLOOR PLAN

The physical layout of a beverage establishment will have a direct relationship to its profitability. Waiters and waitresses must be able to move

FIGURE 6.1   *Buy or Lease?*

BUYING	
Advantages	**Disadvantages**
Buyer accumulates valuable assets.	Equipment will eventually wear out and need to be replaced by the buyer.
Buyer can depreciate a portion of the cost each year.	Buyer assumes the responsibility of maintaining and servicing the equipment.
Interest expense for installment payments is tax deductible.	
LEASING	
Advantages	**Disadvantages**
Lease payments are tax deductible as business operating expenses.	Loss of depreciation.
Lessor may maintain and service the equipment for the lessee.	At end of the lease you do not own the equipment.
Lessor usually supplies brand-new models and updates equipment periodically.	The built-in charge for service may be more than you would otherwise have paid for it.
Service calls on leased equipment are usually given priority over others.	

quickly as they take orders and deliver drinks. Tight aisles and poor table arrangements can slow service and irritate guests.

Your layout should appear friendly and inviting. It should excite guests and make them want to come in and stay longer. Guests must get a pleasing view the instant they enter, because at this moment, the tone of their entire stay is very often set. A good layout will have efficient service aisles and adequate access aisles for guests to approach and leave their tables with relative ease. Restrooms should be reasonably located so as to be seen from most seating areas. Entering guests should have some free space by the entryway from which they can orient themselves and absorb the ambiance for a moment. The bar should be conveniently located so guests will not have to travel a crowded or possibly embarrassing route to sit there. Figure 6.2 provides guidelines for a good layout.

FIGURE 6.2 *Guidelines for Bar and Lounge Layouts*

1. Allow incoming guests to have a view of your lounge that will immediately give them the flavor of the atmosphere

2. Avoid congestion around doorways and traffic lanes

3. Divide large spaces into smaller, intimate areas, through the use of walls, planters, and decorator panels

4. Use contrasting colors or materials to give smaller areas an atmosphere of their own

5. Consider traffic paths to be used when resupplying the bar during busy periods and be sure to avoid inconveniencing guests

6. Provide access aisles for service personnel to deliver drinks

7. Vary your seating clusters, so that you can handle singles, couples, and larger groups of guests

8. Consider using folding doors to create private rooms or to close off empty areas at quiet times

9. Plan cocktail pickup stations so that they create the least distraction or inconvenience to guests at your cash bar

10. Lay out your bar to save steps and to be operable by minimum staff during a slow period

11. Install intercom systems if the bar is connected to other food or lodging facilities

12. Ensure fire exits and safety equipment are easily accessible

13. Ensure restroom signs are visible from most points in the lounge

14. Ensure ample facilities for coat hanging are provided, especially in colder climates

15. Plan bar equipment so as to allow for expansion of business with a minimum of structural changes

16. Arrange bar equipment in efficient work centers to enhance work simplification techniques and reduce stretching, reaching, turning, and other fatiguing movements

17. Incorporate the latest equipment models available in your bar design, which give you the most up-to-date features and put off obsolescence

18. Choose easily cleanable materials for equipment surfaces as well as for floors, walls, and furniture

19. Provide sanitary restroom facilities for employees in your plans

20. Locate service bars as close to the point of service as possible

In designing your floor plan, consider the efficiency of your bar operations. When and how often will your bar have to be stocked? From where will the supplies come? Will guest service be affected at those times? How much product will you carry at the bar? What control routines must be observed in regard to the storage and issuance of beverage supplies? The answers to these questions will determine the location of your storeroom and the size and placement of your bar.

Above all, seating must be comfortable. Few people will tolerate uncomfortable seats more than once. The height of tables and chairs should be conducive to relaxing and to comfortably crossing legs, if desired. The sizes, colors, shapes, textures, and fabrics will all send a message to your guests. Try to select a harmonious variety of seats, booths, banquettes, and tables to maximize the interest level of your décor.

Where the Entertainment Should Go

Do not relegate the entertainment to a particular spot simply because it was considered dead space. The entertainment may not be able to relate to the audience from that spot and, consequently, may not be able to perform at its full potential. Entertainment can entice guests to stay longer or come back again soon, but it can only do this if it is well placed. Consider this issue carefully and locate it where it can be enjoyed by the most guests.

DESIGNING YOUR BAR

When developing a bar design, two basic questions must be answered: "What types of beverages will be served?" and "How many guests will have to be served at one time?" The answer to those two questions will form the basis of any bar layout.

The types of beverages will dictate what equipment is required, the styles of glasses needed, what is needed to prepare specialty drinks (ice cream, coffee, slush), the amount of refrigerated storage needed, and whether to serve draught or bottled beer.

The number of guests will determine the quantity and size of the equipment and the necessary amount of ice, glasses, glass storage space, and serving stations required. And because every beverage begins with a clean, sterile glass, an appropriate glass washing station is always a critical design element.

After equipment sizes and quantities have been determined, the equipment has to be arranged to conform to the flow of the beverages and glasses to and from the serving stations. A serving station is defined as the area and equipment used by a bartender to mix and dispense the variety of beverages required. A small bar can use a single serving station, staffed by one server. The larger the number of guests to be served, the larger the bar and the more stations required for efficient operation.

Oftentimes, in larger operations, a serving station is located at one or both ends of a bar with mixing and dispensing duties shared by the bartender and a server. The ideal bar design takes into account the flow of beverages from the time they are mixed and dispensed, through consumption by the guest, to the return of soiled glasses to be washed, air-dried, and stored.

Again, efficiency is always a consideration. How can a beverage order be prepared with the fewest number of steps? Where should the cocktail mixing station be in relation to the beer dispensing stations and in relation to the POS or the cash register? Will any specialty drinks have to be prepared and what is needed for them? How much floor space in relation to total space available should be dedicated to the bar operation? What is the budget? Will equipment cutbacks be necessary in order to meet budget constraints?

When a bar designer thinks about efficiency, uses common sense, and "acts out" the workings of the operation, it will become clear in the planning stage what equipment is required and where it should be placed. In essence, a good bar layout is no different than an efficient kitchen or office layout.

After a bar layout has been designed, the next step is to select a vendor. That choice will be based on the brand of equipment that will best satisfy the requirements of the design. Equipment may be custom manufactured, but custom manufacturing takes longer to produce, is often more costly and larger than modular equipment.

The modular concept, pioneered by Perlick Corporation, is based on manufacturing products whose final assembly is determined by a customer's specific requirements. With many serving station modules from which to choose, manufacturers can match custom specifications quite

FIGURE 6.3 *A Cutaway View of a Beverage Center*

Photo courtesy of the Perlick Corporation, Milwaukee, Wisconsin

soon after receipt of a customer's layout and order. Serving station modules can be mated with other free-standing cabinets, such as glass frosters, bottle coolers, and glass washers, to create a customized total beverage center like the one shown in Figure 6.3.

Bar equipment is available from a number of sources. However, dealing with numerous suppliers means coordinating those purchases to ensure everything is going to fit and look uniform. Professional buyers prefer to buy as much equipment as meets their needs from a single source. By doing so, they have to deal with only one purchase order and one freight shipment.

EQUIPPING YOUR BAR

All purchases of equipment should be made on the basis of 1) how well they satisfy your operational needs, and 2) how well they serve your patrons' wants and needs. Figure 6.4 illustrates an efficient equipment layout for a large bar.

FIGURE 6.4 Equipment Layout for the Bosier City Riverboat Casino Bar

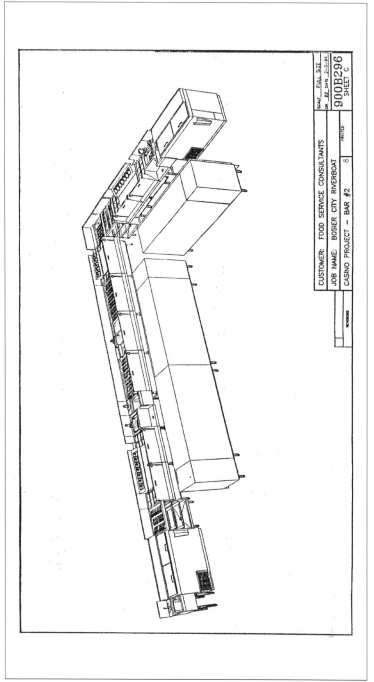

Drawing courtesy of the Perlick Corporation, Milwaukee, Wisconsin

Ask yourself the following questions before making a final purchase decision:

- Do you really need the item? Will it improve your production or service systems?
- Is it the right size? Will it do the job you expect in terms of volume, speed, and quality?
- Is it safe and sanitary?
- Will it blend in well with the rest of your equipment? Does it have a good appearance?
- Can it be serviced easily, and what type of warranty does the seller or manufacturer offer?
- Will it fit in your available space?
- How much will the utility hookups and installation cost? Do you have the required electrical power supply (single phase or three phase), voltage, and water pressure?
- Is the equipment's cost reasonable, in relation to the answers to the above questions?

The size of your bar, its style of service and liquor list, as well as your budget, will determine the type, size, and quantity of equipment you will select. A generic equipment list for a typical bar can be found in Figure 6.5.

FIGURE 6.5 *Typical List of Under Bar and Back Bar Equipment*

Sinks, Three Compartment	Ice Chest with Cold Plate
SS Workbench	Bottle Wells
Speed Racks	Ice Cube Maker
Overhead Glass Rack	Ice Crusher or Flaker
Glass Chiller	Glass Washer
Beer Tap	Glass Storage Rack
Glass Froster	Liquor Display Shelves
Keg Beer Cooler	Back Bar Liquor Storage Cabinets
Bottled Beer Cooler	Speed Gun Soda System
POS or Cash Register	Cocktail Stations
Ice Cream Cabinet	Blenders and Slushers

How to Size Equipment

Sizing of equipment is done by calculating the volume of output needed during your peak periods and finding a model with the appropriate capability. You will have to refer to manufacturers' catalogs. Allow for growth of your business by reducing the manufacturers' claimed output by 30 percent. The following example illustrates the steps involved in selecting an ice maker for a bar.

Selecting an **I**ce **M**aker

Step 1. Examine your liquor list to determine the various types of drinks you will be serving and the sizes of the glassware you will be using

Step 2. Estimate the total number of drinks you will serve on a peak business day by multiplying your expected number of guests by the average number of drinks a guest consumes:

No. of Guests × Avg. No. of Drinks per Guest
= Total No. of Drinks

Step 3. Multiply the total number of drinks (calculated in Step 2) by the average volume of ounces of ice your drinks will contain; convert the total number of ounces of ice required to pounds by dividing by 16 to give you the capacity in pounds that your machine will need to produce on a peak business day:

$$\frac{\text{Total No. of Drinks} \times \text{Avg. No. of Oz. of Ice Per Drink}}{16} = \text{Lbs. of Ice Required}$$

Step 4. Refer to ice maker specifications in equipment catalog and match them up to the capacity that you need

THE BAR

A typical bar has three components: 1) the front bar, 2) the under bar, and 3) the back bar. The front bar is where the guests sit and drink. The under bar is the array of equipment installed on the rear underside of the bar, the production center. The back bar is comprised of the shelving on top, where premium liquors are displayed, and the cabinets underneath, where reserve liquor bottles are stored. Sometimes equipment, such as beer coolers, is built into the back bar. Due to its size, the front bar is usually prefabricated in sections and stained off premises then brought to the establishment for final assembly.

Special attention should be given to the design of the bar, because of its major contribution to the décor and ambiance of an establishment. For appearance and ease of cleaning, bar equipment should be modularized as much as possible.

LOUNGE EVALUATION AND IMPROVEMENT

The best of plans for a successful lounge may require fine-tuning once they are in operation. Keep a constant watch for areas needing improvement. Look for overcrowding, inefficient traffic flow, poor sound control, or bored guests.

The effect of these conditions may be guests leaving earlier than planned and perhaps not returning. Problem areas cannot be ignored. Improving a lounge requires the cooperation of bar personnel. Department meetings should be held to discuss problems, objectives, and solutions. Make a practice of evaluating your lounge periodically.

DESIGNING A SERVICE SYSTEM

The easiest way to design a service system is to put yourself in your guest's shoes and walk through the process of entering a bar or lounge, taking your seat, placing your order, and being served. Then put yourself in a bartender's or waitperson's shoes and walk through the process of greeting the guest, taking their order, turning it in or preparing it, picking it up, and delivering it to the guest.

In your mind's eye you will envision every step of the service system from order taking to cashiering. Imagine it is opening night and a party, of six people just walked through your front door. What happens next? You may have to do this several times, to make certain you haven't left out any details. Success in the public hospitality business hinges on details.

The following questions represent a checklist that should assist you in the planning of a service system:

- How will guests arrive? As pairs, singles, or large groups? This will determine the size of your bar, and the types of seating you will install.
- Will guests arrive by car? If so, do you have adequate, safe parking available?
- Where will guests enter and how will they be greeted? By whom? When? Where?
- Will you use the lounge to accommodate guests waiting to be seated in the dining room?
- Where will your lounge be located in relation to the entrance and to the dining room?
- Who will take the guests' drink orders—a cocktail waitperson or the bartender?
- How will you call waiting guests when their dining room table is ready?
- Will the lounge check be transferred to the dining room, or must guests pay before leaving?
- How will your lounge be subdivided into stations to ensure prompt service?
- Will your lounge have smoking and nonsmoking areas? How will it be divided and ventilated?
- Will your lounge staff wear uniforms or costumes?
- How will the drink orders be delivered to the bartender? Electronically, verbally, or in writing?
- How will servers know when their drink orders are ready to be picked up?
- Will cocktail servers garnish their own drinks?

- What will your policies be for doubles and extra-strong drinks? Will you limit the size or number?
- Who will approve mistakes and voided check items?
- Who will handle any complaints that might arise?
- How will the guest checks be presented to the guest?
- Who will cashier the guest checks?
- Where will charge card sales be processed?
- Will there be a coatroom? Will it be free, coin operated, or have coat checks?
- Where will restrooms be located?
- Where will telephone and dispensing machines be located?

GLASSWARE

Some establishments use a wide variety of glasses in their bars, while others use a very limited selection of glassware. On occasion you may find a bar that uses only one glass for all the drinks they serve. The "one glass fits all" practice is questionable, however, because of its lack of universal appeal. Some glassware has an elegant appearance appropriate for certain settings; other glassware suggests bargain prices or fun and fits well with the desired marketing message of a business.

Selecting Glassware

Below are important factors to consider when selecting glassware:

- Style
- Size
- Strength
- Usefulness
- Cost

The style should be based on your desired image and your guests' expectations. It should be easy to clean, stackable (if that is a desired feature), and in tune with the overall décor and atmosphere of your bar.

Glass sizes should be appropriate for the quantity of liquor you wish to pour into drinks, and that, of course, will be related to the prices you plan to charge. Simply put, you don't need an eight-ounce glass if you are dispensing three ounces of beverage (even with ice).

The strength of a glass is important in liquor operations. Bar glasses are handled much more than most pieces of dining room ware. The speed with which they are handled and washed makes them extra vulnerable to chipping and cracking. Select stock made especially for the hotel and restaurant trade, because it will save you money over the long run.

The usefulness of glassware is something only you can determine. Don't buy glasses that are made for items you do not serve. For example, most pubs do not need fluted champagne glasses.

Try to achieve consistency in your selection of glassware, that is, don't mix fancy with plain, extra large with small, or colors of glassware. The average price of standard bar glassware is about $15 to $18 a dozen depending on size and style. If you are tempted to buy monogrammed glassware, be aware of the risks that accompany it. It costs considerably more, it is not kept in stock by dealers, manufacturers require lengthy lead times to produce it, and it may have little or no resale value if you sell the business.

How Much You Should Buy

How much glassware you should buy will depend on the estimated volume of sales for the various drinks you serve. You will most likely sell more martinis and manhattans than liqueurs in a dinner restaurant. Therefore, you would need more cocktail and rocks glasses than cordial glasses.

Keep in mind that some glasses will be in use on tables, while others will be soiled and waiting to be washed behind the bar. You should have a large enough supply of glasses to handle all contingencies. Most establishments will keep a reserve stock in the back of the house to be used for replacements and very busy occasions. You should plan on breakage of 25 percent or more per year. Once a glass is chipped, no matter how slightly, it must be removed from service.

The sample inventory in Figure 6.6 is for illustrative purposes only; the actual amount of glassware you will need will vary according to your

FIGURE 6.6 *Sample Bar Inventory*

Type of Glass	Quantity
5 oz. Rocks	13 dozen
7 oz. Highball	12 dozen
10 oz. Collins	12 dozen
4 oz. Sour	6 dozen
4 oz. Cocktail	13 dozen
5 oz. Brandy Snifter	2 dozen
12 oz. Beer	13 dozen
6 oz. Wine	12 dozen
2 oz. Sherry	3 dozen
4 oz. Champagne	3 dozen
1 oz. Cordial	3 dozen

type of establishment, the drinks you serve and the sales of each type, the seating capacity, whether you cater large functions, and your glass washing capabilities.

FOOD SERVICE IN THE LOUNGE

Whether to serve food in a bar is a question every operator must decide. In some states, food service is required for certain kinds of licenses. Some patrons enjoy eating at a bar, but others resent people eating beside them when they are drinking at a bar. Your decision depends on the wants and needs of your targeted clientele.

Serving food at a bar impacts on a number of operational issues, such as flow of traffic, ambiance, and seat turnover. The following questions must be answered:

- What will be on the menu at the bar?
- Where will the food be prepared?
- How will the food order be transmitted to the kitchen?
- Who will prepare it?
- When will it be prepared?
- What equipment will be needed to prepare and hold it?
- Who will deliver the food order to the guest?

- Who will cashier the check?
- Who will bus the tables or the bar?

Snacks and casual food are good business builders for a bar, but be aware that the overall cleanliness of a bar can be impacted if provision is not made for regularly scheduled cleanings. Some products, such as peanuts and popcorn, are very popular, but messy. If a regular program of table and floor care is observed, these snacks will not present a problem.

ENVIRONMENT AND DÉCOR

Everything a guest sees, feels, smells, or hears in your establishment is a part of its décor. The instant guests pull on your front door handle, they are experiencing your décor. A massive front door with heavy duty hardware conveys one image, while a small, lightweight front door with economical hardware conveys a totally different image.

So it is with everything in your establishment; colors, sizes, shapes, weights, and textures are all part of your decorating scheme and must be coordinated to produce the image you desire.

Who Should Decorate?

You can decorate yourself or you can hire an interior decorator. There are dangers in doing it yourself, however, even if you have the talent. The main problem is that decorating is a time-consuming and all-encompassing task. As a manager or owner, your time is too valuable to get tied down to one activity for too long. Other parts of your business may suffer and erase any savings from doing your own decorating. Another danger is you may lack knowledge of the most up-to-date materials and techniques that a professional decorator would know about.

Utilizing a professional decorator with whom you work closely is the ideal situation. The owner may have a concept in mind, in which case the role of the decorator is to design around that concept in the best way possible. Or, the owner may commission a decorator to create an original design, transferring a broad range of responsibility for all aspects of the project.

In both instances, the close working relationship is important. In the first instance, the owner must communicate the objectives clearly and completely. To the extent that this is not done, the decorator's ideas rather than the owner's will dominate. In the second instance, it is imperative that the decorator know the monetary limitations of the project. Much time, money, and effort can be wasted if the financial parameters are not established at the onset of the project.

A Clear Message

Your guests should never be in doubt as to what your message is. Everything about your establishment should contribute to your desired image, including:

- Name of the business
- Building design
- Signs (colors, size, type of print)
- Tables and chairs
- Chinaware and flatware
- Tablecloths and napkins
- Carpeting or flooring
- Wall hangings and drapes
- Light fixtures
- Menus (the physical menu)
- Floor plan (table spacing)
- Uniforms
- Plants or other decorative objects

In addition to the above, plan carefully for safety, sanitation, sound control, and atmospheric comfort (heating, ventilation, air-conditioning). Lighting is also important. Coordinate the intensity and color of your lighting along with your fixture styles. Consider all the uses of light, such as background effect, accent, and safety in lighting walkways or directing people.

Basic Design Principles

The wants and needs of your targeted clientele should dictate the type and style of décor. You must develop a theme or concept for your bar and maintain it through every aspect of the atmosphere and décor as well as the food and beverage offerings. Only then are you ready to begin selecting your furniture, fixtures, and appointments.

Below are principles of design to keep in mind as you plan your décor:

- *Balance.* Balance is the quality that gives a room a pleasing sense of togetherness. However, balance will vary as a result of the number of people using the area, so it is important to consider the average occupancy. A crowded bar decorated with dark colors and low lighting may look heavy and imbalanced if it has not been properly decorated.
- *Emphasis.* Emphasis refers to the focal point or center of interest in a room. There should not be more than one focal point or emphasis in a room. The use of walls, partitions, and folding doors in a bar, however, could allow for several different focal points in the same overall space. For instance, in one room the band could be the focal point, while in an adjacent area, the giant-screen TV could be the focal point. Emphasis also can be achieved through the positioning of furniture or contrasts in color, texture, and size and shape. The same tactics used for emphasis also can draw attention away from an unattractive aspect of a room.
- *Flow.* Flow encourages the natural and free movement of the eye from one area to another and can be accomplished through repetition, and progression of sizes. In a bar, the strategic hanging on the walls of paintings or artifacts related to your theme will create flow.
- *Proportion.* Proportion refers to the relationship of one object to another. For example, a large, imposing bar in a small room would appear overwhelming and out of proportion.

Colors

The next step is to determine your color scheme. Psychological experiments have shown that color can affect the mood and behavior of people. Warm colors would be most effective in an informal, lively establishment. Cool colors are better suited to more formal, relaxed places. Warm, neutral colors are often the most appropriate background for bars catering to a more diverse group. Three families of colors lend themselves well to bars: greens, which are friendly in mood and mix well with other colors; browns, which are warm, comfortable, and easy to work with; and reds, which are stimulating and useful as accents.

Floor and Wall Coverings

Selections of fabrics, floors, and wall coverings are also important to the atmosphere of a bar. These items must be chosen with forethought. Consider the type of image you want to convey, as well as upkeep and durability. Synthetic fibers and materials are easily maintained. The most common floor coverings are wood, carpeting, brick, stone, and ceramic or vinyl tile.

Wall coverings may be rigid, such as plaster, brick, and wallboard, or flexible, such as paper and cloth. Vinyl-treated papers are well suited for a bar or lounge because they are washable and can be very decorative.

Furniture

Be it classic, contemporary, or modern, the furniture, along with other appointments, is going to play a major role. As always, it is necessary to analyze your clientele and the reasons they come to your bar.

A lounge with live entertainment and dancing needs quite different furnishings than a quiet, conversational-type bar. Where there is dancing, there will be less room (and probably less need) for large, comfortable pieces of furniture. Many people will be mingling or dancing, thereby necessitating less area for sitting and more area for movement. On the other hand, a place that is trying to convey an image of intimacy should have plenty of tables, comfortable chairs, and cozy booths. The style and arrangement of furniture serves to reinforce the image of a bar.

Lighting

Poor or inappropriate lighting can destroy the whole effect of a bar. The color of your lighting plays an important role in creating the image you desire. White light, for instance, shows colors as they really are but does not add charm. Cool color lights, such as blue, give a feeling of more space to the room but add a chilling effect. Warm color lights, on the other hand, can soften the chilling effect by dulling the cool colors.

The position of lights is also important. Light sources that are located below eye level will tend to make a place seem more intimate and friendly. The higher the source of light, the more formal is the effect rendered. Small direct lights will emphasize a focal point; large diffused ones tend to unify a space.

Troubleshooting Tips

There are an infinite number of possibilities for decorating and creating atmosphere in a bar. The best approach is to narrow down the choices by carefully defining your concept and desired clientele, and then using professional decorators. Unless you have particularly strong skills in this area, your time will be better spent on other planning or managerial responsibilities. Figure 6.7 will help you focus on important issues when improving atmosphere and décor.

FIGURE 6.7 *Tips for Improving the Atmosphere of a Bar*

Problem	Negative Effect	Suggested Improvements
Faded, drab, or dirty looking colors	Causes dull, listless feeling on part of guests	Use new paint, murals, hanging plants
Damaged chairs and tables	Gives guests the impression your establishment is unsuccessful	Refinish or replace chairs and tables

FIGURE 6.7   *Tips for Improving the Atmosphere of a Bar (Continued)*

Problem	Negative Effect	Suggested Improvements
Bright room	Lacks coziness of a friendly lounge	Adjust rheostats; repaint walls with intimate colors; soften walls with accents; replace light fixtures, if necessary
Large room	Creates feeling of being lost in a crowd	Group tables to give impression of intimacy; use divider walls, planters, and screens to break up the huge room look
Ceilings too high	Causes heat loss, increases noise levels, and makes room seem impersonal	Lower the ceiling or install sections of false ceiling; hang interesting objects
Overcrowded feeling	May cause restlessness or irritation at being bumped accidentally or constantly having to move for someone to pass	Rearrange existing tables and, if possible, use an adjacent room for overflow seating
No variety in presentation of drinks	Diminishes guests desire to reorder	Change liquor list more often; highlight different drinks; set up attractive wine displays to stimulate interest; feature holiday and seasonal drinks
Standing guests crowded around tables or booths	Disrupts atmosphere; gives guests feeling of being intruded upon	Contain by rope cordon or dividers or portable screens
Overheated lounge	Causes drowsiness and irritation	Lower the thermostat and improve ventilation, but avoid drafts in larger rooms
Moody or impatient employees	May cause irritation and dislike of the establishment when bad moods are evident to guests	Identify problems and strive for a positive work environment
Untidy appearance and unprofessional attitudes on part of staff	May cause apprehension on the part of guests	Supervise the activities of the lounge more closely; conduct training sessions to improve attitude; install a dress code or buy new uniforms to improve appearance; be more selective when hiring
Employees favoring certain guests	May cause irritation to others due to delays in serving	Discuss at training sessions

A *ctio* **n G** *uidelines*

✓ Choose a concept, considering your location.

✓ Identify your target market and describe their wants and needs.

✓ Plan equipment around your food and beverage offerings.

✓ Consult an equipment dealer or food and beverage consultant for professional assistance in laying out your equipment.

✓ Utilize the services of a decorator, unless you have professional competencies in the interior decorating field and can afford to devote the time required.

7

OPERATING PROFITABLY

Every dollar lost unnecessarily in the course of doing business flows directly to the bottom line, and reduces profits by a dollar. To operate a bar profitably, one must keep a tight control over all *profit centers* of the business. A profit center is a segment of the overall operation, an activity, that can increase or decrease profits. Typically, there are seven profit centers in a beverage establishment. If a bar also sells food, it would have two additional profit centers—menu planning and food preparation. The seven profit centers are:

1. Purchasing
2. Receiving
3. Storing
4. Issuing
5. Production
6. Service
7. Cashiering

Purchasing the right products, in the proper quantities, and at favorable prices is important. Of equal importance is securing the products in controlled storage and using them properly. Liquor is a tempting product that should not be left sitting about the premises. It should be stored and logged into an inventory book or computer system as soon as it is received. Likewise, when a bottle is issued, the withdrawal should be recorded. Standard drink recipes should be used by all bartenders to ensure a consistent taste and liquor content for all drinks. Finally, to close the control loop, all monies collected should be accounted for.

INVENTORY TURNOVER RATE

Like any retail enterprise, a bar cannot afford to carry dead stock. Money tied up on storeroom shelves gathers dust, not interest. In certain instances, however, such as when fine wines and exotic drinks are featured on the menu, a bar may intentionally carry a number of slow-moving items in stock for merchandising reasons. Nevertheless, a manager can exercise a high degree of inventory control by calculating a turnover rate for the other 80 percent of the stock.

Your *inventory turnover rate* is the number of times your inventory is turned into cash, within a given period of time. Put another way, it measures how long it takes to sell the goods you buy. The method for calculating an inventory turnover rate is shown in Figure 7.1.

In the preceding example, the beverage inventory was turned over about every 12 days. Turnover rates may vary by season. The optimum turnover rate is the highest number of times that cover your operations adequately between reorders, along with a small safety margin for unexpected increases in business.

It is recommended that all bars keep some sort of written record of items ordered from distributors, and compare shipments with purchase orders. The receiver can then quickly spot substitutions or incorrect items. This procedure prevents controversy about orders and deliveries, and it serves as part of an audit trail for cost control. The first documentation is the purchase order, an example of which is given in Figure 7.2.

Your Initial Inventory

Three categories of spirits are carried in most bars—bar brands, call brands, and premium liquors—distinguished by cost and quality. Bar brands, also called well brands, are the least costly liquors, and are used

FIGURE 7.1 *Calculating Inventory Turnover Rate*

Step 1. Calculate the cost of the beverages consumed

Beginning Beverage Inventory 1/1/20___	$ 5,000
Plus: Beverage Purchases 1/1–1/31	13,000
Total	18,000
Less: Ending Beverage Inventory 1/31/20___	5,500
Cost of Beverages Consumed	$12,500

Step 2. Calculate the average beverage inventory

Beginning Beverage Inventory 1/1/20___	$ 5,000
Plus: Ending Beverage Inventory 1/31/20___	5,500
	$10,500

$10,500 ÷ 2 = $5,250 Average Beverage Inventory

Step 3. Calculate the inventory turnover rate

$$\frac{\text{Cost of Beverages Consumed}}{\text{Average Inventory}} = \text{Inventory Turnover Rate}$$

$12,500 ÷ $5,250 = 2.38 times a month

when a guest does not request a particular brand. Accordingly, drinks made with bar brands are priced somewhat lower. Call brands are those liquors that people ask for by name, and premium brands are the top-shelf items that guests request by name.

It is not possible or feasible for a bar to carry every product available, but it is essential for a bar to carry a reasonable variety of liquors in order for guests to have a choice. For example, there are literally hundreds of Scotch whiskeys produced, yet a bar could have a good representation of the various types and quality ranges with only 8 to 12 brands on its shelves. Other types of liquors do not require that many brands to be stocked to offer a good representation of the product. Ideally, if a bar does not carry the specific brand a guest may request, the bartender should be able to offer an acceptable substitute.

The quantities of each brand to be ordered for your initial inventory will depend on the wants of your clientele. Liquor sales representatives will be eager to help you get started. A good salesperson, who wants your continued business, will not overload you.

FIGURE 7.2 *Sample Purchase Order*

DATE				No. 1185
		The West Coast Bar & Grill		
		PURCHASE ORDER		
		Please furnish the following—All carrier's charges prepaid.		

Qty.	Unit	Description	Unit Price	Amount

Received by: _____   Purchasing Agent: _____

INVOICE MUST ACCOMPANY MERCHANDISE

When selecting distributors, your focus should be on the popularity of their brands, their terms of payment and discounts, promotional assistance, the availability of free wine lists and promotional materials, and their frequency of deliveries.

In evaluating brand popularity, distinguish real demand from artificial demand. You should observe whether the requests for a product you don't carry are coming from a few people or many. On occasion, an overzealous salesperson has been known to have friends patronize a newly opened establishment and repeatedly order the product the salesperson is trying to sell to the bar in order to create what seems to be a large demand for it.

Maximum and minimum inventory levels should be established for all items, based on their actual sales history, and should be adhered to. There is little point in buying several cases of a slow-moving product to obtain a discount of a few dollars if an alternative use of the money would yield an equal or greater return.

HOW TO SELECT YOUR INVENTORY

The most important consideration when selecting inventory is your clientele. Who are they? What will they expect when they patronize your establishment? When will they arrive—in the daytime or at night? What is their purpose—business lunch, entertainment, after-work relaxation? The answers to these questions will indicate the types of drinks your guests will tend to order.

It is not unreasonable to limit your stock of certain beverages and suggest an alternate brand. The goal of inventory management is to carry the brands that are needed to keep your guests happy, while not tying up your money needlessly. Occasionally, some premium brands are carried mainly for prestige value and, as long as it's not overdone, that practice is acceptable. Following is a list of the alcoholic beverages carried by most full service bars:

- Scotch Whiskies
- Canadian Whiskies
- Blended Whiskies
- Gins
- Brandies
- Fruit-flavored Brandies
- Beers and Ales

- Irish Whiskies
- Bourbon Whiskies
- Vodkas
- Tequilas and Rums
- Cognacs
- Liqueurs and Cordials
- Wines

The reason bars carry three levels of liquors—bar brands, call brands, and premium brands—is to provide a choice for all tastes and all pocketbooks. Bar brands are very acceptable products but usually have little or no guest recognition. In some establishments, drinks made with bar brands constitute the bulk of the sales volume.

In addition to your spirits, you will need to carry an adequate inventory of wines and beers. The optimum size of a wine inventory will vary according to the bar's clientele and type of food served. Beers are usually carried in bottle or keg form. The selection of brands is heavily influenced by regional preferences. However, if your bar caters to tourists and traveling businesspeople, your decisions might need to include national preferences. At least one dark beer should be carried in restaurant bars, and one or more light beers are recommended for diet conscious people. Today, most bars also will carry two or more nonalcoholic beers.

Figure 7.3 is a sample of a typical Liquor Inventory Sheet. The amount of backup stock carried in a liquor storeroom or wine cellar will depend on several factors:

- Frequency of deliveries
- Storage space available
- Availability of certain products
- Budget for liquor inventories

KNOW YOUR METRICS

The liquor industry has switched to the metric system. This makes little difference to the average guest because a 750 milliliter bottle looks like a fifth and a 1.75 liter looks like a half gallon, but a bar manager should know the difference. Here is how the old and new sizes compare:

Old Sizes	New Sizes
Miniature—1.6 oz.	50 ml.—1.7 oz.
Half-pint—8 oz.	200 ml.—6.8 oz.
Pint—16 oz.	500 ml.—16.9 oz.
Fifth—25.6 oz.	750 ml.—25.4 oz.
Quart—32 oz.	1 Liter—33.8 oz.
Half Gallon—64 oz.	1.75 Liter—59.2 oz.

It is very important for inventory control purposes to select the proper sizes for your bar operation and to stick with those sizes. Mixing of sizes can lead to inaccurate valuation of stock when extending inventory totals. Most bars prefer to buy 750 milliliter bottles, because they fit into speed racks and are easier for bartenders to handle.

FIGURE 7.3 *Sample Liquor Inventory Sheet*

The West Coast Bar & Grill *All 750 ml. unless otherwise stated*					
	Quantity on Hand			**Unit Cost**	**Value**
Item	**Store-room**	**Bar**	**Total**		
BOURBON					
Beam's Choice					
Old Grand Dad					
Wild Turkey					
TENNESSEE WHISKEY					
Jack Daniels No. 7					
Jack Daniels No. 7 Green					
BLENDED WHISKEY					
Fleischmann's Preferred					
Seagrams 7 Crown					
SCOTCH					
King William IV					
Chivas Regal					
Dewar's					
RUM					
Bacardi 151 Proof					
Mr. Boston Light Rum					
Bacardi Amber Label					
Myers Original Dark					
Mount Gay Eclipse					
BRANDY & COGNAC					
St. Charles Brandy					
Courvoisier VS Cognac					
Hennessy VS Cognac					
FLAVORED BRANDY					
Leroux Apricot Brandy					
Arrow Blackberry Brandy					
Jacquin Peach Brandy					
GRAND TOTAL INVENTORY					

Note: The use of product names is for illustrative purposes only and is not intended as a recommendation, nor is the list of liquors comprehensive.

RECEIVING, STORING, AND ISSUING LIQUOR

All alcoholic beverages should be checked in and put away in a secure storage room immediately after deliveries are received. All items received, including bar supplies and promotional items and gifts, must be recorded. Use a form such as the sample Receiver's Report in Figure 7.4. The receiver should check to make sure that the proper brands and bottle sizes were delivered. Cases should be opened, counted, and checked for breakage before the delivery slip is signed by the receiver. Only competent employees of legal age should be allowed to receive and handle alcoholic beverages.

On occasion, a delivery may arrive without the appropriate delivery slip. In such an event, a Merchandise Received without Bill form, like the one in Figure 7.5, should be filled out with a description of the merchandise received and the signatures of the delivery truck driver and the receiver. This form confirms that the goods were actually received and avoids the possibility of confusion at a later date

If incorrect merchandise has to be returned, have the truck driver sign a Request for Credit Memo, similar to the one in Figure 7.6, when you relinquish the goods. In the past, when such documentation was written by hand, it was possible to simply erase a returned item from a delivery slip and re-total it. Today, with computerized billing, it does no good to simply change a bill, the data must be entered into the computer. The Request for Credit Memo is proof that an incorrect item was indeed returned for credit. It also serves as a reminder to the accounting department to make sure the credit comes through at the end of the month.

A liquor storeroom should be well lighted, ventilated, and dry. It should have a secure door lock, and keys should be issued to only one or two people who have a need to access it. Storeroom shelves should be spaced far enough apart to accommodate the tallest bottles, standing up. The uppermost shelf should be easily reachable. In addition, every product should have a specific storage location on the storeroom shelves that corresponds to its position on the inventory sheet. This significantly reduces the time required to take inventory.

FIGURE 7.4 *Receiver's Report*

The West Coast Bar & Grill
RECEIVER'S REPORT

No.: _____
Date: _____
Received by: _____

Purveyor	Qty.	Unit Size	Description	✓	Unit Price	Amount	Total Amount	Distribution	
								Direct to Bar	To Liquor Storeroom

FIGURE 7.5   *Merchandise Received without Bill*

				BII860

The West Coast Bar & Grill
MERCHANDISE RECEIVED WITHOUT BILL
Please send us a bill for the following items:

From: _____   Date: _____
_____

Quantity	Item	Amount

	Total

Delivery Driver: _____   By: _____

FIGURE 7.6   *Request for Credit Memo*

				BII860

The West Coast Bar & Grill
REQUEST FOR CREDIT MEMO
Please send us a credit memo for the following:

To: _____   Date: _____
_____

Quantity	Item	Amount

	Total

Delivery Driver: _____   By: _____

FIGURE 7.7 *Bar Requisition Form*

The West Coast Bar & Grill **BAR REQUISITION**	
Date: _____, 20___	
_____ **Department**	
Issued to the undersigned:	
No. 1234	**Signed:** _____ **Department:** _____

A record should be kept of all withdrawals from the storeroom. One method is to use a Bar Requisition Form, like the one in Figure 7.7. At the end of each shift, a bartender gathers all the empty liquor bottles at the bar and fills out a requisition form for replacements. The requisition slip is turned in to the storeroom, and the bartender receives a bottle-for-bottle exchange for the same brand and size. The sample Stock Record Card in Figure 7.8 provides another method for recording inventory activity in the storeroom.

Following a storeroom procedure not only controls the storeroom, but it also keeps the *par stock* at the bar at the desired level. The term *par stock* refers to the total number of bottles that should always be present at the bar. It is usually the number of bottles required for a day's business, without having to restock. In some very busy bars, with limited space, restocking must be done at the start of each shift.

FIGURE 7.8 *Stock Record Card*

The West Coast Bar & Grill
STOCK RECORD CARD

Item: _____

Purveyor: _____

Article: _____   Size: _____   Unit Cost: _____

Location: _____   Unit: _____   Cost per Oz.: _____

Max.: _____

Min.: _____

Date	In	Out	Bal.	Date	In	Out	Bal.	Date	In	Out	Bal.

YOUR BEVERAGE SALES REPRESENTATIVES

In noncontrol states, liquor, wine, and beer are sold by private business enterprises in the same manner that food products are sold. Their salespeople usually call on bars on a weekly or biweekly basis. Because no single distributor carries all brands, it is normal to buy from several distributors. You should arrange for salespeople to call on you at a mutually convenient time.

Salespeople can be valuable sources of information on the local popularity of the various types of beverages. They also can help you plan an opening inventory. With their assistance, you can keep current on price increases, product shortages, new products, special promotions, merchandising aids, and special discounts. When evaluating the services of a distributor, consider the following questions:

- Does the distributorship offer adequate delivery service?
- Does it require minimum orders?
- Will it split cases?
- Does it have to substitute products frequently due to being out of stock?
- What types of discounts does it offer?
- Does it supply sales promotional material?

Let salespeople know what your philosophy is on inventory turnover so that they can work with you. Also, let them know what your marketing concept is; for instance, do you want to be able to make every conceivable drink or just the popular drinks? The better you communicate with salespeople, the better they will know what you want, and the better they will be able to serve you.

Finally, realize that salespeople are just like all other people. There are some very good ones and some not so good ones. When you have a choice between distributors, focus on the dependability and willingness of salespeople to help you as you get started.

USING STANDARDIZED DRINK RECIPES

Guests want a consistent drink every time they order, no matter who makes the drink. Variations in taste, size, and type of glass among bartenders are not infrequent occurrences in some bars. These inconsistencies may occur from drink to drink, or from bartender to bartender. You can avoid this problem by standardizing the recipes of all your drinks. The main advantages of using standardized drink recipes are:

- They ensure high-quality drinks all day, every day.
- They are useful when breaking in new bartenders.
- They reduce overpouring.
- They allow a more accurate accounting of bar sales.

A standardized recipe is a set of instructions that tells your bartender what your house policy is in regard to the type of glassware to be used, the quantity and type of ingredients, and the method of preparation. The success of standardized drink recipes is based on always using the products and portion sizes specified. Shown below is an example of a standardized recipe.

MARTINI ON THE ROCKS

7 oz. Rocks glass/almost filled
    with ice cubes
2 oz. Gin
½ oz. dry Vermouth
Stir and serve with a sip stick
    and olive or twist

File cards make excellent drink recipe cards. Every bar should have an easily accessible set of their standardized recipes, for reference by bartenders. Most professional bartenders will have their own set of drink cards that can be modified where necessary to conform with the house recipes. The advantage file cards have over bound recipe books is that additions can be made easily, without upsetting the alphabetical arrangement. The recipes may also be stored in a POS system, from which drink costing sheets can also be printed. Recipes that you may develop to be featured as house drinks should be carefully tested before being served to guests. A set of 80 popular drink recipes is included in Appendix C at the back of this book.

Overpouring Is Expensive

If a bar uses standard drink recipes and trains its employees well, it should not have a serious problem of overpouring. Many bars, however, do not, and consequently, many bartenders do as they please—some overpour thinking they will get bigger tips from guests.

Overpouring is a very costly practice that should be eliminated. The following example illustrates just how expensive it can be, even when only a small amount is overpoured in each drink.

Assume the following:

1. A bartender overpours ¼ oz. of liquor in every drink.
2. Your bar volume is about $2,000 a day.
3. Drink prices average $4.50 a drink.
4. The average cost of a 750 ml bottle of liquor is $12.

Calculation:

About 444 drinks are sold daily ($2,000 ÷ $4.50 = 444 drinks)
444 drinks × 0.25 oz. = 111 oz. lost daily due to overpouring
111 oz. = 4.37 bottles (750 ml bottles contain 25.4 oz.)
4.37 bottles × $12 (avg. cost of bottle) = $52.44 lost daily
$52.44 × 365 days = $19,141 potential annual cost of overpouring

That $19,141 should be in the bottom line of your income statement. When a bartender overpours, your profits are being given away, and you are not even getting credit for the gift. The greater concern, of course, is that unless the practice is stopped, larger amounts may be overpoured in the future.

Some bars take overpouring so seriously, they give a free-pouring test to their bartenders every two weeks. If bartenders fail a test, they are given one week to regain their pouring accuracy. If they fail the second time, they are dismissed.

THE IMPORTANCE OF SUPERVISION

It is easy to not look for problems when things appear to be going well. For that reason, some bar owners lose sizable sums of money each year without realizing it is happening. This type of operator may never know just how great the business might have been, had better control been maintained over it. Profit leaks can occur from mistakes, waste, and dishonest practices. To plug the leaks, control procedures should be in place in all profit centers, and close supervision should be maintained to ensure that the procedures are being carried out.

Following is a list of 34 situations that can cause a bar to lose profits—all are correctable:

1. Not keeping the liquor room locked and taking other precautions to prevent theft and misuse
2. Not safeguarding the keys to the liquor storeroom by issuing them to only one or two supervisory persons whose duties require access to the storeroom
3. Not following up on credits for merchandise backordered or returned because of damage
4. Buying excessively that results in carrying too much stock in relation to sales volume, tying up working capital that could be used for other investment opportunities
5. Not taking advantage of discounts and promotional deals, which amounts to overpaying for bar stock
6. Not checking invoices and payments against receiving records to detect any shortages, backorders, and incorrect prices
7. Not buying liquors in consistent bottle sizes (750 milliliter or 1.75 liter), and consequently applying incorrect values when taking inventory
8. Inaccurately recording additions to and subtractions from inventory in a perpetual inventory book, bin cards, or into a computer

9. Mishandling of products leading to breakage, and not having a management person verify breakage when it occurs

10. Not making spot checks of the par stock at the bar to ensure that the total bottle count (full, partially full, and empty bottles) is what it should be

11. Not taking a complete physical inventory at frequent intervals to calculate the pouring cost percentage and to verify the accuracy of the perpetual inventory figures

12. Allowing products to spoil due to improper storage conditions, such as moisture, excessive heat or cold, and exposure to intense light for long periods of time

13. Failing to take corrective action quickly when the cause of a problem is discovered

14. Failing to properly orient and train new employees

15. Not assigning clear responsibility for control of the liquor supply to one management person

16. Not using a system of forced issues to get rid of dead stock or very slow moving items when cash flow needs improvement

17. Bartenders not adhering to standard recipes and overpouring liquors

18. Not properly pricing drinks to yield the desired pouring cost percentage

19. Bartenders unprepared and too slow to capitalize on rush hour potential

20. Bartenders drinking stock and giving free drinks to other employees and friends

21. Theft of products by employees and delivery people who enter the establishment

22. Bartenders not using standard glassware for drinks

23. Bartenders trying to run a mental tab, instead of collecting for each drink as served, then collecting improper amounts

24. Not providing standard measuring tools for bartenders to use, or bartenders failing to use these tools when mixing drinks

25. No standard house policies established by management and explained to all bar personnel

26. Not covering and refrigerating garnishes overnight, allowing them to spoil

27. Not keeping daily record of drinks sold to compare with the quantity of liquor consumed that day
28. Carelessness at bar resulting in excessive spillage and breakage
29. Overstaffing, by scheduling extra bartenders and wait staff when not needed
30. Not keeping adequate sales records to track guest preference trends
31. Making wine and liquor lists so complicated they confuse guests and dampen sales
32. Failing to advertise special promotions and events to the extent allowed by law
33. Failing to meet guests' wants and needs in regard to the liquors offered and the atmosphere of the establishment
34. Failing to gather feedback from guests to assess how pleased they are with the establishment

Dishonest Practices

Observers of the retail industry indicate pilferage is a major problem and acknowledge that employees represent a significant segment of the pilferers. The retail beverage industry is no exception. Products or services can be given away, overcharged or undercharged for, or charged for but not recorded. The list of possibilities is lengthy. How then can management deal with the problem? The answer is to hire the best employees possible, maintain tight controls, and supervise closely.

It has been said that 25 percent of all people are completely honest. Because of their beliefs or moral fiber, they are not interested in self-gain by committing dishonest acts, and they resent people who are so inclined. Another 25 percent are to varying degrees attracted by or constantly in search of dishonest opportunities. The remaining 50 percent of people fall somewhere in the middle. They are basically honest, but if constantly tempted, some will be swayed toward the dishonest end of the spectrum.

Obviously, the object of a good security program is to sway the neutral group toward the honest end of the spectrum. Tactics include removing temptations, controlling products and sales, setting policies and standards for conduct, and letting people know their actions are being observed. These are important deterrents to dishonest practices; however, the first line of defense is to interview applicants thoroughly and check references, which is discussed in Chapter 9.

ENTERTAINMENT

Entertainment is often a business builder. Good entertainment can attract new guests and keep your existing guests from drifting to competitors. A common misconception, however, is that entertainment will automatically improve business volume. To the contrary, ineffective entertainment can be a financial drain on your business. Not all entertainment is good, and cost is not an assurance of quality or results. When considering adding entertainment, you should ask yourself the following questions:

- What type of entertainment best fits your format?
- Do you have excess seating capacity? Can you accommodate additional volume with your present facilities?
- Are your competitors using entertainment successfully? If so, what kind?
- Are your guests asking for a certain type of entertainment or, in the case of a new bar, will your target market expect it?

Three types of entertainment may be considered for a bar: individual performers, bands, and mechanical background music. Mechanical background music includes jukeboxes and tape and digital sound systems. It is the least expensive type of entertainment and, in the case of a jukebox, can be an income producer. It should be noted, however, that if a jukebox's selections or the volume at which it is played are not pleasing to your clientele, you may lose guests.

Individual performers, such as piano and guitar players, are the next least expensive. If they are good, they can add a uniquely pleasant quality to a barroom. Some performers, with a loyal following, are capable of attracting their fans wherever they work. Their popularity in bars emanates largely from their personalities and their ability to relate to audiences. It is important to audition this type of performer carefully before hiring.

The range of talent on the market is broad, and a poor choice of entertainer could actually have a negative effect on business.

Bands can be good attractions if they are popular. But the more popular they are, the more expensive they are. In general, they are more feasible for establishments that have a large seating capacity and a price structure that can absorb the band's high cost. Bands also require setup space and numerous electrical outlets.

When dancing is instituted, entertainment must be monitored very carefully, because while people are dancing, they are not eating or drinking. Cover charges can offset the cost of entertainment, with the caution that the clientele must perceive the entertainment to be worth the price of admission.

Another consideration is the size of your dance floor. Too small a floor discourages your patrons from dancing, and too large a floor wastes valuable sales-generating seating space.

Entertainment should be evaluated regularly by asking the following questions:

- Is the entertainment increasing sales?
- Is it attracting the type of clientele you seek?
- Are profits increasing as a result of entertainment?

An analysis sheet for evaluating entertainment is shown in Figure 7.9. It can serve as a useful measure to compare the results entertainers achieve and to suggest when corrective action is warranted.

It is important to know your clientele—who they are, what they expect, and how they think. For many smaller bars, mechanical background music supplied by a jukebox or a leased music system is perfect. Music can set the mood of your bar, and a wide variety is available—intimate mood music, melodic light classical music, top 40 pop music, and heavy-metal rock music, to name but a few. In any case, your choice should be based on what your target market wants.

Your Break-even Point for Entertainment

Assume you have excess capacity. That is, on certain nights of the week you have many empty seats. This concerns you because your overhead

FIGURE 7.9 *Weekly Entertainment Analysis Sheet*

WEEKLY ENTERTAINMENT ANALYSIS SHEET

Week of ____	Name of Entertainer	1 Total Revenue	=	2 Food Sales	+	3 Beverage Sales	4 Total Cost of Entertainment	=	5 Cost of Entertainment	+	6 Advertising and Any Other Costs	7 Ratio (%) Entertainment Cost to Food and Beverage Sales (4/1=7)

costs go on whether you have a half-filled house or a full house. Consequently, you could significantly increase your business volume without incurring any additional overhead costs. To attract more people to your bar on those slow nights, you decide to offer entertainment and hire a four-piece band. You run an advertisement in the local newspaper to let the community know you have entertainment. (If you had other related expenses, you would add them to the calculation.)

Your main concern at this point is that the entertainment, at the very least, must pay its own way—breakeven. If it does not do that, it will not have accomplished its purpose of increasing business, and is, in fact, a further drain on profits and must be changed or terminated.

Figure 7.10 assumes you operate with a 20 percent pouring cost and illustrates how you can calculate a break-even point for entertainment.

It is important to note that the break-even point is the amount of *additional* sales that must be obtained in order to pay the cost of the entertainment and the related advertising, and will not necessitate raising drink prices. If sales increase by $7,500, the bar will have taken in just enough to breakeven. There would be neither a profit nor a loss at this point. Your hope is that as the entertainment catches on, sales will increase substantially above the break-even point and profits will rise.

FIGURE 7.10   *Calculating the Break-even Point for Entertainment*

Step 1. Determine the total cost of the entertainment

Cost of Entertainment ($1,600 per night for 3 nights)	$4,800
Cost of Advertisement	1,200
Total Cost Related to the Entertainment	$6,000

Step 2. Establish your contribution margin

100% – Pouring Cost Percentage (PC) = Contribution Margin

100% – 20% = 80% (contribution margin)

Step 3. Calculate your break-even point

Total Cost of Entertainment ÷ Contribution Margin = Break-even Point

$6,000 ÷ 0.80 = $7,500

$7,500 = Break-even Point

INSPECTING AND MAINTAINING EQUIPMENT

Another key to making profits is reducing equipment repair costs. An effective maintenance program will more than pay for itself. It can help avoid accidents, reduce downtime, and add dollars to your profit line. Equipment failures often mean disappointed or inconvenienced guests, frustrated or injured employees, and harried managers. It makes sense to keep your equipment in top shape. Aside from the fact that repair calls are expensive, it is hard to find good service people.

The following five steps will help you institute your own inspection and maintenance program:

Step 1. The first step in developing a maintenance program is to explain to all employees the need for the program and the benefits it will bring. Unless everyone believes in the program and cooperates, it will not work well. Most people respond to safety benefits and labor-saving features, so stress those points.

Step 2. Develop a file folder for every piece of major equipment. Each folder should contain the name of the product, the manufacturer's name, the model year and style of each piece of equipment, the warranty form, the service agency's name, a record of service calls with costs and dates, the manufacturer's specification sheets, and the owner's operating manual. While a number of smaller items can be combined in one folder, it is preferable to keep a separate folder for each major item.

Step 3. It is important to formalize the program by developing a checklist for inspections. With a list, no piece of equipment is overlooked, and each piece of equipment undergoes proper inspection.

Step 4. Develop a set of easy to understand and accessible maintenance procedures for each piece of equipment. It is a good idea to keep three copies of all procedures—one for employee use, a second one for the manager's file, and a third copy as a spare (you can be sure one will get lost).

Step 5. Assign the responsibility for the inspection of equipment to a specific person. The frequency and extent of inspections should be clearly understood. There should be no doubt about the process of reporting the results of inspections and following up on corrective actions.

Instituting an equipment maintenance program lets employees know that the company cares, and they will strive to ensure its success. Many attempts at reducing breakage and malfunctions of equipment fail because employees are not properly motivated to cooperate. This is clearly a case where management must set the tone by doing its part to ensure success of the program.

Technology Is Helping

The role of the computer in operating profitably is constantly changing. Many of the controls and procedures discussed in this book can be enhanced by computer applications. It should be noted, however, that the output of a computer is only as reliable as the raw data entered into it, and attentive care must be taken to ensure accurate data gathering.

Technology has improved the task of gathering data, as discussed in Chapter 2, with electronic devices that can assist with tedious tasks such as inventory. But management must still understand the underlying factors that contribute to high costs and expenses in order to take effective corrective actions when costs are out of line.

A*ction* **G***uidelines*

✓ Obtain a liquor list from a liquor store or dealer and select an initial inventory.

✓ Create an inventory sheet that includes all of the items in your initial inventory for taking physical inventories.

✓ Develop a perpetual inventory book (using a three-ring binder) with a separate stock record card dedicated to each brand of liquor carried in stock.

✓ Demonstrate your understanding of beverage turnover rates by calculating the turnover rate for a bar with the figures shown below:

Beginning Inventory 11/1	$3,000
Purchases 11/1–11/30	$8,400
Ending Inventory 11/30	$3,700

✓ Develop an equipment list and a maintenance sheet for each item on the list.

8

THE BAR AND BARTENDING

Good drinks, service, and ambiance are what make a bar popular, but sound policies and standards are what make it profitable. Bartenders must be well trained and supervised to ensure that house policies are being adhered to. They must also be supplied with the necessary tools, equipment, and products to perform as expected.

Customers want their drinks to be consistent, regardless of which bartender makes them; they want the same glass size, ingredients, and garnish every time they order their favorite drink. To achieve such consistency, a bar should have a standard recipe and glass for every drink served. Many bars cover this in their training manual, but high-quality drinks and consistently good service begin with a competent bar staff.

STAFFING THE BAR

The ideal candidate that every bar would like to hire is a person with professional bartender training, several years of experience in a reputable establishment, and alcohol responsibility certification. Unfortunately, most applicants will not have these ideal credentials.

Some bars and restaurant chains do their own training; however, those that do not have qualified instructors or the time to give in-house training should hire individuals who have been trained by a state-licensed, professional bartending school. Licensed schools give supervised hands-on training in a real bar setting and require students to pass a competency test with a substantial score before receiving a certificate. These applicants will usually have received alcohol responsibility training as well, and should have documentation to verify that training. Interviewers should question applicants carefully, and should be alert to exaggerated claims of training.

The experience of an applicant also should be scrutinized carefully, because some experience can be laden with bad habits. If a résumé shows many jobs held in a short span of time, it may be a sign of a problem. Unless stated, ask why the applicant left each job and consider the reputation of the previous employers. It can tell much.

High-volume bars often will hire barbacks to assist bartenders. The barbacks will prepare mixes, cut fruit, make garnishes, fill ice bins, remove trash, and draw beers. Some bars will gradually train the most promising ones to be bartenders.

BAR POLICIES SHOULD BE CLEAR

Employees need to know what is expected of them in situations that require decisions. A clear set of policies will give them the confidence they need to respond properly to matters as they occur. A concise statement of policies should be documented and posted on a bulletin board or kept in a manual that is easily accessible to all staff. Changes in policies should be announced immediately and, from time to time, compliance with policies should be evaluated to ensure they are being carried out. It is important that management set an example in adhering to policies, because any wavering on its part will lead to uncertainty as to the importance of a policy. Following are examples of five areas for which a bar should have policies:

1. *Code of conduct.* This code should reflect the desired image of the establishment and might include the following:
   - Never leave the bar unattended during business hours without first consulting a management person

- Never express dissatisfaction with a tip to a patron
- Never use profane language with, argue with, or make suggestive advances toward a patron
- Never talk inappropriately about one patron to another

2. *Emergency evacuation.* Employees should know what to do, where to go, and how to assist patrons to safety in the event of a fire or other emergency.

3. *Robbery policy.* Make certain that employees who handle money, and are most likely to be targets, know how to respond should such an event occur. They should understand that it is important to do nothing to aggravate the situation; they should stay calm, cooperate, and not put themselves at risk.

4. *Identification.* A bartender should check valid IDs of persons who do not clearly appear to be at least age 30.

5. *Personal appearance.* Bar staff must be dressed and well groomed, as prescribed in the company manual, while on duty.

PREPARING TO OPEN THE DOORS

The key to a smooth running bar operation is preparation. Everyone should know what they are supposed to do, when they are expected to do it, and how it should be done. If a busy bar is not totally prepared before the first customer steps in, it may struggle through an entire shift trying to get caught up, running out of supplies and apologizing to customers. Following are common duties of bar staff for each shift throughout a day.

Typical routine of a daytime bartender. This includes:

1. Oversees cleanup and vacuuming by porters (unless cleanup is done at night, immediately after closing)
2. POS terminal or cash register is cleared by a supervisor who then issues a bank to the bartender. Bartender counts bank to verify amount, and inserts the money into cash drawer.
3. Checks and restocks the bottled beer box and the draft beer keg supply

4. Counts number of empty bottles, and marks number and brand on a requisition sheet to be used for drawing replacement bottles out of the storeroom
5. Turns in empty bottles to the liquor storeroom (or wine cellar) and draws out full bottles, in a bottle-for-bottle exchange
6. Checks and restocks supply of napkins, soda tanks, sugar, stirrers, straws, packaged lemon mix, and fresh fruit for garnishes
7. Opens faucets for a few minutes to run out stale water
8. Runs one or two gallons of hot water down drain of draft beer grill to prevent clogging
9. Prepares packaged drink mixes, as necessary, to cover the shift
10. Wipes down stainless steel and bar surfaces
11. Stocks ice bins with crushed and cube ice
12. Cuts up fruit and fills dispensing trays with required garnishes
13. Inspects the bar and lounge for overall cleanliness and appearance
14. Inspects himself or herself for appropriate dress and appearance
15. Opens the bar for business, and serves customers with a smile

Typical routine of a night bartender. This includes:

1. Before taking over, makes sure all bar glasses that may have been washed in the kitchen are returned to the bar
2. Double-checks all supplies and restocks the bar, as necessary, before the day bartender leaves
3. POS terminal or cash register is cleared by a supervisor and the night bartender is issued his or her bank. Bartender counts bank to verify the amount.
4. Makes out a change request, obtains the necessary breakdown of bills and coinage to meet the cashiering needs of the shift, and inserts bank into register drawer
5. Starts work, mixes drinks, serves customers, and handles cash
6. At end of shift, stores all empty bottles in cartons
7. Washes and puts away all remaining glasses
8. Takes apart glass washer and allows brushes to dry overnight
9. Takes care of general cleanup—stainless steel, sinks, and bar; vacuuming usually done by porters in the morning

Typical closing duties. These include:

1. Lock all doors from the inside to prevent anyone from entering
2. Check restrooms and other areas for slow patrons
3. Drain sinks, one at a time, to prevent backflow
4. Place fruit and perishable items in refrigeration
5. Secure cash in safe or authorized location
6. Adjust thermostats to night temperature
7. Recheck premises and turn off interior lights, except for safety lights
8. Turn off exterior lights and sign
9. Set burglar alarm and test before going out the door

Weekly bar routines. These include:

1. Clean out beer box thoroughly to remove any broken glass and wipe up spillage
2. Clean out wine and liquor cabinets
3. Flush out beer lines. This is usually done by a professional cleaning service, but with the right equipment and training it can be done in-house. Clean lines are essential for serving high-quality draft beer.

HANDLING CASH AND CHARGES

While newer bars have sophisticated cash registers that eliminate most of the problems associated with older ones, care must be taken to handle every transaction properly. It takes many dollars of additional sales to make up for a customer lost due to a mishandled monetary transaction.

A business cannot assume their new hires were properly trained by a previous employer. POS systems and cash registers vary widely, and every bar has its own way of doing things. For these reasons, training in the following areas must be given to every new employee who does cashiering:

- Handling cash sales
- Running a tab
- Handling charge sales

To establish accountability for shortages and mistakes, each bartender should work from his or her own bank and cash drawer. A bank is an amount of money in bills and change issued at the start of a shift to be inserted into the cash drawer and used to make change during the shift. At the end of the shift, the bartender empties the cash drawer and turns in the money, which should equal the sum of the starting bank plus the receipts for all of the cash sales cashiered during the shift, as recorded by the register. If the amount of cash turned in is less, there is a shortage for which the bartender is accountable. Charge sales are considered separately and are reconciled with the printed receipts.

If the establishment has a multidrawer register, two bartenders may work from one cash register, provided that each starts with a separate bank and uses a separate register key to access his or her own cash drawer. Cash sales should be collected after each drink or round is served. If customers ask to run a tab and pay at the end, an account must be opened.

Tabs are handled differently from bar to bar, depending on the type of establishment it is and the type of clientele it attracts. A high-energy bar that caters largely to transients or younger people who often come in groups to party will deal with tabs in a much different way than a bar that has an established clientele and no history of people forgetting to pay their bill when leaving. It is common practice in barrooms to request a major credit card to open a tab. Once an account is opened on the cash register, subsequent drinks can be added to the previous balance by pressing the previous-balance key on a cash register or its counterpart on a point of sale (POS) screen. When the party is ready to leave, the card owner receives the bill, signs it, and the card is returned.

In restaurants, when a party is ready to go from the barroom into the dining room, most will collect for the bar tab in the barroom, however, some will transfer the bar tab to the dining room. Running tabs is not a one-size-fits-all matter; every management must decide which procedures are most appropriate for their particular clientele.

ABOUT DRINKS

No one knows how many drinks exist, they come and go; some are only regionally popular, and others are the signature drink of a single bar or restaurant. Most of the recipes in lengthy drink books are long out of date and rarely ordered. For these reasons, it is not necessary for a bartender to know every drink that was ever concocted. It is important, however, for them to keep up with new drinks that are emerging in the region they serve.

A compilation of 80 tested drink recipes is listed in Appendix C at the back of this book. Be sure to add your regional favorites to the list to create a set of standardized recipes. There are also numerous Internet sites that list hundreds of drink recipes, but caution should be exercised when considering them for adoption—some may not have been tested adequately. It is wise to cross-check Internet recipes against other sources to ensure their accuracy. A few of the more popular Internet sites include the following:

- The Webtender (*www.webtender.com*)
- idrink.com (*www.idrink.com*)
- BarFliers.com (*www.barfliers.com*)
- BARTV (*www.barTV.com*)
- DRINKSMIXER.com (*www.drinksmixer.com*)
- BarNone Drinks (*www.barnonedrinks.com*)

Some establishments not only require new bartenders to adapt to their house recipes, they quiz them periodically to make sure they are all pouring the same quantities and mixing drinks the same way. This practice ensures consistency and supports their cost control system.

In bars where management does not supply bartenders with a printed set of house-approved recipes, they should specify a standard size pour, a standard glass, and a standard method of mixing drinks in their new employee orientation. A good drink is not overloaded with alcohol. Pouring according to a tested recipe will produce a quality, well-balanced drink, and, equally important, it is a responsible business practice.

When bartenders get an order for a new drink that they are not familiar with, a proper response would be, "I'm sorry sir (or ma'am), that's not a drink we get call for here, but if you can tell me how it's made, I'd be happy to make one for you." If the customer does not know how it is made, as is often the case, the bartender can help the person make another choice. A bartender should never try to fake it; those drinks usually come back with a complaint.

DRINK CLASSIFICATIONS AND PRICING

Drinks are commonly grouped in categories that relate to a meal, such as before-dinner drinks or dessert drinks, or to a common ingredient, such as cream drinks. Beyond that, they may be subdivided price-wise, according to the number of liquor ingredients they contain, such as one-liquor drinks or two-liquor drinks. Drink prices also may vary according to the quality of the liquor requested. A martini made with a top-shelf gin will be priced higher than one made with a common well brand. Fortunately, today, the prices of drinks with their many variations can be programmed into a POS system or a computerized cash register and be recalled from memory in hundredths of a second. These electronic systems have virtually eliminated the pricing errors of the old days. The pricing of drinks is discussed in detail in Chapter 11.

LIQUOR POURING TECHNIQUES AND SYSTEMS

There are basically three ways to dispense liquor: free pouring, measured pouring, and electronic-system pouring. Each has its place, as well as its advantages and disadvantages.

Free pouring is a learned technique for manually dispensing liquor without using a measuring device. It is based on a mental count (such as one thousand, two thousand, three thousand) that times the flow of liquor into a glass. It is a fast way to pour and can be reasonably accurate, because slight overpours and underpours should average out to the desired pour, but, it is a good idea to give bartenders a free-pouring test, whenever the bar's pouring cost percentage (PC) is creeping higher than desired. With experience, a bartender will soon learn to free pour without actually counting, and will sense the difference between the rate of flow of thinner liquors and the denser liqueurs. Free pouring is often used in high-volume bars where customers tend to come in droves at peak periods. Its advantages are it is entertaining and fast. Its disadvantages are it requires monitoring and, if not done properly, can cost a bar profits and disappoint customers.

Measured pouring is simply using a handheld measuring device to dispense liquor. Theoretically, the liquor should be measured accurately. In reality, bartenders frequently pour over the line on the glass. The most useful measuring device is the plastic hourglass shaped one that has multiple lines on it—gradations for one, two, and three ounces on one end, and fractions of an ounce on the other end. Because most recipes require more than one measurement, this type of device is more accurate than the traditional single-line shot glass. The advantages of measuring, when done right, are it can be accurate and customers can see what is going into their drink. The main disadvantage is it is much slower and, therefore, not as suited to high-volume bars and peak business periods.

Electronic liquor dispensing uses computer-driven systems that dispense the ingredients of a drink. At the push of a button, say, the Martini button, the ingredients—1½ ounces of gin and ½ ounce of dry vermouth—are determined in microseconds from a database. They next are pumped in perfect quantities out of the appropriate bottles, which are stored behind a wall, and delivered through plastic flowlines to a dispensing head at the bar, where a bartender with glass in hand is ready to receive them.

Beyond the basic system, there is a variety of enhanced systems available, ranging up to complex ones that integrate each drink sale with inventory and cost control systems. Their main advantage is excellence in controlling costs. Their disadvantages are their high cost of installation and their appearance of being impersonal. Although, as was shown in Chapter 2, Motoman offers a robotic bartender, RoboBar, that attracts friendly customer interest.

MIXOLOGY

The mission of a bartender should be to deliver high-quality drinks consistently and in a timely manner. Quality is achieved by using good recipes; consistency is achieved by executing the recipe properly each time; and timeliness is achieved by being organized and knowing the tricks of the trade.

An efficient order in which to make drinks is to start with the ones that create the least mess. These are usually the drinks that are the easiest to make as well. Set up your glasses so that you can pour all drinks that require a common liquor ingredient at once. This saves steps and reduces bottle handling. Then proceed to the more complicated ones and the ones for which your tools must be washed immediately after making each drink. The last ones to be made are those that will cool off or go flat if they stand around too long. The order is as follows:

- Straight shots and liquor on the rocks
- Highballs (liquor with a mixer)
- Fruit juice and sour drinks (e.g., collinses and sours)
- Liqueur drinks (with strong flavors that can migrate to other drinks)
- Hot drinks (coffees and toddies) and beer

Always handle clean glasses by the base or stem. Never stick your fingers into soiled glasses in order to pick up more than one at a time. The appearance is distasteful to customers and the practice can transmit harmful germs.

Every drink should be served in a clean glass and with a fresh napkin and stirrer or straw. Because discounts are not given for subsequent drinks, there is no justification for giving anything less than what the customer got with his or her first drink.

BARTENDING TOOLS

A bar should supply a complete bar kit for each bar station, and keep at least one spare kit on hand in case a tool breaks or is lost. A shaker cap can fall onto a hard surface, lose its round, and become a leaker; a mixing glass can chip or break during a shift; or a lost tool can go undiscovered until nearly opening time—all of which can be unnerving. Many bartenders will lock their tools in a cabinet at the end of their shift to prevent these occurrences. Figure 8.1 shows a sampling of bar tools, many of which come in a variety of sizes and also have plastic alternatives.

The most necessary tools are:

- *Mixing glass.* A heavy, clear glass in which stirred or shaken drinks are mixed with ice.
- *Shaker cap.* A stainless steel cap that fits tightly over the mixing glass for shaking a drink; always strain a shaken drink from the shaker cap because it keeps the drink colder.

FIGURE 8.1 *An Array of Bar Tools*

- *Speed cup.* A small stainless steel version of the shaker cap that fits over a highball or collins glass.
- *Strainer.* A stainless steel device used to strain a drink from the shaker cap into a stemmed cocktail glass.
- *Bar spoon.* A long, stainless steel spoon with a handle that can be used to stir, a bowl that is used to scoop, and a spiral design on the handle that can be used to agitate a drink when rubbed back and forth between a bartender's palms.
- *Ice scoop.* Stainless steel scoops of various sizes are used to fill glasses with ice. (Note: Never use a drink glass to scoop ice out of an ice bin because the glass may break from a thermal reaction. Also, do not hand-scoop ice because it is unsanitary.)
- *Ice pick.* The six-prong ice pick is useful in breaking up clumps of ice in the ice maker bin.
- *Jiggers.* Used to measure the liquor ingredients of a drink. They are available in stainless steel and plastic, and come in a variety of sizes. The plastic ones with multiple gradations are recommended.
- *Fruit squeezer.* Used for squeezing the juice out of a section of fruit because it is neat and shows well.
- *Corkscrew.* Some bartenders prefer the wing type at the bar, but most bartenders and servers use the pocketknife type. It folds, has

a small knife blade for cutting seals, a sturdy screw to pull out corks, and a bottle cap remover.

- *Funnel.* Has many uses at the bar, particularly when preparing mixers and simple syrup.
- *Garnish fork.* Used for spearing and releasing olives, cocktail onions, and cherries in a drink; showy, but most bartenders use bar picks.
- *Pourers.* A liquor-dispensing device that fits into the neck of a bottle to control the rate at which the liquor will be dispensed. Some have smaller diameter spouts that pour slower; others are speedier. Also available are automatic measuring pourers.
- *Knife and cutting board.* A sharp paring knife and a polyethylene cutting board (less porous than wood and approved for food use).

GLASSWARE

A glass is more than a vessel that holds liquid—bar glassware can be an effective marketing tool. Glass sizes and shapes can upgrade a drink, particularly drinks with vibrant colored ingredients. Battery-lighted Lucite serving trays are being used in many bars to dramatize the brilliant beauty of an assortment of colored drinks as they pass by on their way to a table. Glassware is discussed in greater detail in Chapter 6.

Figure 8.2 illustrates how the size of glassware affects the yield from a half barrel keg of beer. The approximate yields shown assume each glass of beer is properly drawn by the "down the side of the glass" method, has a one-inch head of foam, and the keg is completely emptied. The temperature of the beer and pressure of the system may also vary the yield. Consult with your beer distributor for the specifics of your particular system.

GARNISHES

The only purpose of a garnish is to glamorize a drink, therefore, carefully selected fruits and vegetables should be used to make them. They should be refrigerated when stored overnight, and sorted out before being put back into service. To avoid overwhelming a drink, they

FIGURE 8.2 *Draught Beer Glassware*

	SHELL	SHAM PILSNER	FOOTED PILSNER	TULIP GOBLET	SCHOONER	HOUR GLASS	GLASS STEIN	CERAMIC STEIN
			NO. GLASSES PER ½ BARREL					
7 oz.	330	418						
8 oz.	294	345	305	315				
9 oz.		305		305				
9½ oz.	264							
10 oz.	250	264	248	293	330	264		
11 oz.						233		
12 oz.		214			256	209	198	
13 oz.						190		
14 oz.					203			
15 oz.						172		
16 oz.								161

should be cut and sized properly and balanced with the size of the glass used. Garnishes to have on hand include:

- *Olives.* Use pitted, green olives.
- *Cherries.* Use pitted maraschino cherries.
- *Cocktail onions.* These are tiny onions that do not have the odor and acid of a regular onion.
- *Lemon twists.* Use a strip of lemon peel, about ¼ × 1½ inches, which when twisted over a drink emits oils and acids that give it a pleasant flavor and scent. It should be rubbed around the rim of the glass before being dropped into the drink.
- *Lime wedges.* Use a triangular section of a lime that has had its ends trimmed off and has been halved and quartered lengthwise, then sliced crosswise into wedges. The wedges must be squeezed and deposited in a drink to enhance it.

- *Celery stalks.* Use medium to small sized, trimmed, and unbruised stalks. Hearts of celery are best.
- *Pineapple.* Chunks of well-drained canned pineapple are acceptable for bars that have little call for coladas or tropical and oriental drinks.
- *Nutmeg.* Sprinkle on Brandy Alexanders.
- *Cinnamon.* Cinnamon curls (not powder) are the proper form of this spice, often used to steep in hot drinks.
- *Whipped cream.* Use for decorating coffee drinks.

HOW TO PREPARE COCKTAILS

On the Rocks
1. Fill Rocks glass with ice cubes
2. Add ingredients
3. Stir ingredients in glass with sip stick
4. Garnish, as applicable
5. Serve with a cocktail napkin

Straight Up
1. Put scoop of ice cubes into mixing glass
2. Add ingredients
3. Stir with handle of barspoon or shake ingredients, and strain into cocktail glass
4. Garnish, as applicable
5. Serve with a cocktail napkin

Tips
- To easily separate a metal shaker cap from a mixing glass after shaking a drink, you should give the shaker cap a sharp tap at the frost line with the heel of your hand.
- The use of half-and-half as a substitute for heavy cream and milk is widespread today because of its lower calories than heavy cream and its acceptance by patrons.
- You should use crushed ice when blending drinks; cubes will strain or burn out an electric blender.

TEAMWORK PRODUCES BETTER PROFITS

It is essential for management to work closely with the bar staff, and to be constantly looking for ways to improve the operation, be it by replacing faulty equipment, relocating electrical outlets in order to save footsteps, scheduling better to handle rushes, adding work stations, or whatever is necessary. As with any specialty, bar operations have their own vocabulary and terms. It improves communication when management personnel are familiar with the terminology used by the bar staff. Appendix B includes a comprehensive list of common bar terms. Employees will work harder and be happier when they feel management is in touch with their concerns, and consequently, they will earn greater tips and the establishment will earn greater profits.

An Interview with a Veteran Bartender

Q. How did you enter the bartending field?

A. I went to bartending school after high school, and was able to get a bartending job right after that. I've been a bartender since then, for 22 years.

Q. What advice would you give to prospective bartenders today?

A. Learn properly, and be flexible when applying for your first job. Just try to get your foot in the door. Continue to learn from the experienced bartenders when you're on the job. Don't take short cuts; stir and shake drinks properly. Customers like it, it's entertaining. And don't neglect any customers, treat them all equally. Keep up on the news and sports, and have a funny story ready for someone who needs cheering up.

Q. What's your approach to shutting off someone?

A. I explain to them that I don't like to do it, but I have to watch out for my job, and I have to watch out for the business; we could lose our license, and we don't want them to get sick or have an accident. When I put it that way, they seem to understand.

Q. Have drinkers changed over the years?

A. *Yes. They're more responsible now. Everyone knows the consequences of getting a DWI. Many groups will have a designated driver.*

Q. Has bartending changed over the years?

A. *Yes. Bars are strict about checking IDs now. Some bars won't serve certain strong drinks after 11 PM. New types of equipment make the job easier. Point of sale (POS) systems save a lot of footsteps and speed up service. New liquor products are available, and new drinks are being invented every day.*

Q. What are some of the hottest new drinks?

A. *It varies by region, but the Washington Apple is hot now (½ ounce Crown Royal, 1 ounce Sour Apple Pucker Schnapps, 1 ounce cranberry juice). And, of course, the new martinis. Next year there will be a bunch of new ones.*

Patrick Doughan has been a professional bartender, bar manager, and bartending instructor over the past 22 years.

Action **G**uidelines

✓ Using the drink recipes contained in Appendix C as the basis for a set of standardized recipes, add local favorites in your area to create a complete set.

✓ Develop a set of bartender routines for each shift.

✓ Draft a set of bar policies.

✓ Create a list of questions for use when interviewing bartenders.

9

MANAGING YOUR EMPLOYEES

For many bars and restaurants to-day, the number one problem is finding good employees. Constant recruiting and training is time consuming, expensive, and often destabilizing to operations. Yet, some owners and managers are slow to address the underlying reasons why employees do not stay longer in certain jobs.

Certainly there always will be seasonal and temporary jobs to be filled and jobs with limited upward mobility, but there are things that management can do to slow down the revolving door dilemma plaguing some establishments.

When a business bases its success on the performance of its employees—training them well, providing them with the right tools, paying them competitively, and offering some level of health benefits to regular, full-time employees—everyone wins. The business thrives, its guests are better served, and the employees develop a sense of satisfaction in their work.

GUEST SERVICE COMES FIRST

In the bar and restaurant field, it is mainly servers who have contact with guests, but every employee in a business must understand he or she has a role in guest service. They must understand how their jobs fit into the process of satisfying guests.

The manner in which a server approaches a guest, presents information, answers questions, and demonstrates an appreciation for the guest's patronage has a great influence on how much that guest will spend and how often they will return. Equally important, however, is the work done by other employees. A poorly prepared meal, a soiled glass, or a messy restroom may disgruntle a guest to the point that they will not return. Instead, they try another place, and if they have a pleasant experience, they continue to go there.

One bad experience can cause the loss of a significant amount of revenue. For example, if a lost guest patronized a bar three times a week, and spent an average of $15 each visit for food and drinks, that represents a revenue loss of as much as $23,400 over a ten-year period. What makes the matter more acute is that no one knows how many guests are lost, because they usually do not complain—they just disappear.

HOW TO GET THE MOST FROM YOUR EMPLOYEES

A good management team will first identify its objectives, then determine ways to accomplish them; developing sound policies and conveying them clearly to all employees. Everyone will then know exactly what is expected and how to achieve the desired results. Getting the most out of employees begins with hiring the best people you can afford, and

- training them properly;
- providing the right equipment and work spaces they need to do their jobs well;
- letting them know that you care about how things are done and are aware of what happens;
- soliciting ideas for improvement and making them aware that they are important to the organization;
- letting promising employees know that there is opportunity for advancement when openings occur; and
- supervising them carefully.

LABOR TURNOVER RATE

The rate at which employees terminate employment has an impact on the profitability of a business, because the cost of replacing employees is very high. The true cost of high labor turnover often is not realized by employers and includes the following:

- Cost of time for the exit interview
- Possible unemployment compensation tax increase
- Cost of advertising the job openings
- Hidden cost of lost production due to the declining morale of the remaining employees who have to pick up the slack
- Cost of time for interviewing
- Cost of training new employees
- Cost of inefficiencies and products wasted while the new employees learn their jobs

Labor turnover rates can be calculated by dividing the number of employees terminated during a given period by the number of jobs in the organization. Multiply by 100 to convert this ratio to a percentage. For example:

$$\frac{\text{No. of Employees Who Terminated} \times 100}{\text{No. of Jobs}} = \text{Labor Turnover Rate}$$

For example, if The West Coast Bar & Grill had 8 of its 30 employees terminate employment last year, its labor turnover rate would be 26.7 percent, as follows:

$$\frac{8 \times 100}{30} = 26.7\%$$

PAYROLL ANALYSIS

Another labor-related concern is staff productivity. The hospitality business is very vulnerable to seasonal ups and downs, and employers must react quickly to changes in sales to protect their profitability.

Employee productivity can be measured as it relates to 1) the number of guests served per employee (covers per employee), 2) sales per employee, and 3) sales per hour worked. These measures of productivity, which are illustrated in Figure 9.1, may be calculated as follows:

Covers Served ÷ No. of Employees = Covers per Employee
Sales ÷ No. of Employees = Sales per Employee
Sales ÷ Actual Hours Worked = Sales per Hour Worked

INITIAL INTERVIEWS

Care should be taken to hire the best people you can afford. Employment applications can be an important tool in this process, but be sure to avoid legal pitfalls concerning the type of information that may be asked. Generic employment application forms may be purchased, or you may design your own. If you choose to do the latter, consult your nearest Department of Labor office to make certain you are not violating any employment rules.

Interview job applicants thoroughly to avoid hiring people with undesirable traits. Following are some examples of behavior exhibited by an applicant that would warrant additional scrutiny:

- Displays impatience at answering questions
- Avoids giving specific answers
- Has an untidy appearance
- Is noticeably impolite
- Becomes overly friendly or takes liberties, such as touching objects on your desk
- Gives the appearance of having an active addiction problem
- Has a record of past employment problems or has unexplained gaps in the chronology of his or her work experience

Be careful not to prejudge any of the above situations as appearances can be misleading. Try to determine if the questionable characteristic has an acceptable explanation, or if it would be an obstacle to the proper performance of the job sought.

FIGURE 9.1 *Illustration of a Process for Analyzing Weekly Payroll*

WEEKLY PAYROLL ANALYSIS

Date Week of	Sales for Week	Covers Served	No. of Employees	Actual Hours Worked	Payroll	Covers per Employee	Sales per Employee	Sales per Hour Worked
Nov. 9	$20,400	2,354	18	720	$2,450	130.8	$1,133	$28.33
Nov. 16	18,540	2,138	19	730	2,468	112.5	976	25.40
Nov. 23	17,480	2,082	20	790	2,595	104.1	874	22.13
Nov. 30	18,910	2,073	20	800	2,550	103.7	946	23.64
Dec. 7	23,750	2,445	21	810	2,675	116.4	1,131	29.32

EXIT INTERVIEWS

The purpose of having exit interviews is to determine if there are reasons for an employee's departure that might have been avoided or that signal necessary changes. Sometimes an employee will leave a job because it is boring. Knowing this, management may be able to reconfigure the job to make it more interesting. On occasion, employees will leave a job because they see another employee doing something of which they disapprove and do not want to become involved. Exit interviews can sometimes reveal information that an employer could not otherwise obtain.

NEW EMPLOYEE ORIENTATIONS

Inform new employees immediately what you will expect of them and what they may expect of you. Orientation sessions are essential if you wish to convey information in a clear and consistent way to all employees. The content of the sessions are dependent on the type and size of an organization, but certain kinds of information are of interest to all employees. Figure 9.2 is a checklist of orientation topics that might be covered, as applicable.

It is also important to list any and all actions that may result in termination of employment. You may want to address the following situations in your new employee orientations or in a posting in an employee area:

- Drinks or uses drugs on the job
- Steals
- Is uncooperative with superiors
- Treats a guest improperly
- Is unable to work with others
- Gives away drinks or other products

Some items will only need to be touched upon, while others may require an explanation. In any case, the new employee should be given an opportunity to ask questions. A thorough orientation at the time of employment may avert employee problems at a later date.

FIGURE 9.2 *Sample Orientation Checklist*

ORIENTATION CHECKLIST

- History of the establishment
- Who the owner is
- Who the management personnel are and who the employee reports to and takes orders from
- Hours—regular work week, when and where posted
- Vacation policy—how much time and when
- Fringe benefits—insurance, sick days, etc.
- Meals, if applicable—when and what items
- Compensation—rate per hour and what deductions
- When payday is
- Tardiness policy
- Absenteeism policy
- Smoking policy
- Coffee break policy
- How training will occur—when, where, and by whom
- Advancement policy
- Overtime policy—if allowed, who authorizes it
- Tip reporting policy
- Lost guest check policy
- Breakage policy
- Partial pay or loan policy
- Dress code

- Who will supply uniforms and how many
- Who will launder uniforms
- Deposits for uniforms, if required
- Appearance of employee— fingernails and cleanliness
- Policy on jewelry and hairnets
- Policy on types of shoes (for safety considerations)
- Employee evaluation policy—how, when, and by whom
- Probationary period and warning policy
- Detailed tour of establishment— including where to park, which restrooms to use, and where to enter and leave
- How to call in, in case of emergency—when and who to call (with phone numbers)
- Personal behavior
- Personal phone call policy
- Policy on patronizing the establishment before or after work hours
- What to do in case of accidents or fire
- Use of safety guards on equipment
- Portion control policy
- Holiday work policy
- How to handle guest complaints

TRAINING YOUR STAFF

A common mistake when a new employee starts on a job is to simply turn them over to a present employee for training. The problem with that practice is the bad habits of the present employee are also passed on to the new person.

Studies have shown that when current employees without training know-how are asked to teach a newly hired person how to do a job, only 80 percent of the information tends to be passed on intact. Moreover, the information continues to erode when successive new hires are trained by existing workers who themselves received only 80 percent of the information.

If present employees are to train new workers, they should be given at least a minimum of instruction on how to do so. A four-step method of training has been used very effectively in industry and is applicable to any training situation. The four steps are show, tell, let do, and check back:

1. Show the employee how to do the task by demonstrating it.
2. Simultaneously tell the employee what you are doing and why you are doing it.
3. Let the employee do it once, under supervision. If the employee does it right and has no questions, allow them to continue on their own.
4. Check back soon after to make sure the employee continues to do the task properly.

This technique is effective with such tasks as cash register training, where there are a number of small, but easy to forget, steps involved. Even new bartenders with experience must be familiarized with your equipment and policies before they start to work independently.

Providing the proper equipment is management's responsibility. It is inexcusable for bartenders to be overpouring or putting out inferior drinks simply because they lack the proper tools. The physical arrangement of a bar is also important. A poorly laid-out bar can prevent a bartender from working efficiently.

Training meetings can be useful for communicating information, getting feedback, and stimulating employees by making them feel recognized, but they are useful only if the presenter is well prepared and there is a need for having a meeting. Following an outline prevents wandering off track and encourages brevity. Likewise, smaller meetings with participants who have a common interest, such as the bar staff, the kitchen staff, and the dining room staff, and even subsections of these, are more productive than larger meetings.

The use of training aids can strengthen a presenter's delivery and reinforce an employee's understanding of the information. The Education Foundation of the National Restaurant Association (*www.nraef.org*) produces excellent audio/visual aids on sanitation, safety, food preparation, alcohol responsibility, dining room service, and other topics, and may be purchased by bars and restaurants. They also have a series of certificate programs with training materials available.

HOW TO GAIN YOUR EMPLOYEES' COOPERATION

It is possible for an owner or manager to lead a somewhat normal life in the bar or restaurant business if they have loyal and cooperative employees. Regrettably, many operators are not so blessed, largely because they do not realize cooperation must be won, not dictated.

Following are six ways to win cooperation:

1. *Make your employees want to cooperate with you.* Let them know what your policies and objectives are. Let them know how they can personally benefit by working toward the accomplishment of your objectives. Appeal to their professional pride and desire to be on a winning team.

2. *Do not expect unreasonable results.* Set a fair challenge, but above all, be realistic.

3. *Be open-minded to employees' suggestions and views.* This shows you are concerned and sympathetic even when you have to say no.

4. *Do not hesitate to give well-earned praise.* If it is honest praise, the employee knows he or she deserves it. Acknowledging a good job, particularly on an undesirable task, is a good way of winning the employee's cooperation the next time you need to get a tough job done.

5. *Avoid arguments with employees.* Time has a calming effect—use it. Let the employee tell his or her side of the story and acknowledge that you heard it. Then arrange a time for discussion. Just a few minutes are often enough time for tempers to settle. Even the thorniest problems can be dealt with more easily when the parties involved are in control of their emotions.

6. *Do not hesitate to admit an error on your part.* It will not change your status or authority. Instead, it will humanize you in the eyes of your staff.

HOW TO IMPROVE EMPLOYEE MORALE

Low employee morale will inevitably result in poor work habits, waste, accidents, and, consequently, a loss of profits. Every aspect of a job contributes positively or negatively to the morale of the worker doing it. An effective manager will keep close watch on the morale of his or her organization and take corrective action quickly if it declines. Some ways to improve morale are listed below:

- You should not ignore rumors.
- You should discuss the impact of any proposed changes that will affect employees.
- Let your employees know how they are doing. Employees often believe they are overlooked when they do something well, but are immediately notified when they make a mistake. Try to eradicate that notion by giving them positive feedback as well as suggestions on how to correct any deficiencies.
- You should be firm, but fair—make reasonable assignments and enforce rules in an impartial manner.
- You should work through your chain of command—don't undercut your supervisors by throwing your weight around or by dealing directly with subordinate employees.
- You should try to find out what every employee's strength or special skill is, and, when possible, give him or her opportunity to use it.
- You should provide employees with the environment to do a good job. This not only includes the proper tools but also sanitary and safe equipment, good lighting, sound control, and physical comforts (such as rubber floor mats on a hard tile floor).
- You should be responsive to your employees' concerns. You may not agree with them, but do not try to avoid them. If the complaints are valid, they won't go away. In any case, explain the reasons for your thinking.

KEEP THE LINES OF COMMUNICATION OPEN

It is a good practice to discuss problems with your bar personnel on a regular basis. Issues such as high cost percentages, adverse guest comments, or a critical health inspector's report can be better solved in an atmosphere of cooperation, where employees are allowed input.

Create an environment that will allow your employees to communicate with you. Give them a chance to offer constructive ideas at meetings—but keep the meetings brief and businesslike. Have a written agenda ready—look organized, but not intimidating. Think of the meetings as a two-way street with information flowing from you to them and from them to you. It will be up to you to direct the discussion in order to keep it in a productive channel.

CONDUCTING STAFF MEETINGS

Meetings are effective only when they are preplanned and carefully executed. The leader must convey the purpose of the meeting quickly, otherwise, it will quickly degenerate to idle conversation. Figure 9.3 is a sample checklist to refer to when conducting meetings. You should review it periodically.

FIGURE 9.3 *Sample Checklist for Efficient Meetings*

- Do I have my material well organized?
- Do I seem to speak to one person, or do I make eye contact with everyone?
- Do I try to solicit views from employees who are less apt to speak out?
- Do I appear alert and enthusiastic?
- Do I set a good example with my speech and professional behavior?
- Am I supportive to employees who offer constructive suggestions?
- Do I avoid placing blame and embarrassing an employee in front of others?

BEWARE OF HIDDEN AGENDAS

Try to eliminate any fears, jealousies, antagonisms, or misunderstandings among employees. These conflicts detract from an employee's performance and may be visible and objectionable to guests. When such a situation occurs, bring both parties together, confront the issue, and let them know how it is affecting their work. Seek agreement from both parties on the resolution of the problem.

Management's challenge is to instill a spirit of cooperation among all employees. A few useful strategies for dealing with employees are

- be friendly, but firm;
- listen patiently to both sides of a story before judging;
- be as tactful as possible;
- explain thoroughly the reasons for your decision;
- never argue in front of guests or other employees; and
- try to end discussions on a positive note.

JOB DESCRIPTIONS

Job descriptions are used for many purposes; most notably, they are used for identifying necessary tasks and proper procedures. Rarely, however, do nonmanagement employees receive a job description when they are hired. This is unfortunate because the new employee is the person who could benefit most from knowing what is expected. A job description also can serve as an excellent checklist when training a new employee.

A sample job description for a bar manager is shown in Figure 9.4 for illustrative purposes. As with all jobs, the duties of a bar manager will vary depending on the size of the operation, the type of bar, and the degree of autonomy the owner grants the manager. Frequently, as in the case of small bars, the owner is also the manager.

FIGURE 9.4 *Sample Job Description*

BAR MANAGER

Summary

Responsible to the owner. Oversees the day-to-day operations of the bar (both front of house and back of house). Responsible for implementing company policies and performing the following duties: purchasing liquor, wine, and beer; hiring and training new employees; supervising and motivating staff; performing control functions; and maintaining a high level of quality and service in all aspects of the operation.

Responsibilities

1. Performs all assigned duties and responsibilities according to company policies and reports to the owner in a timely and efficient manner

2. Researches and purchases products necessary to satisfy guests' wants and needs and the sales objectives of the establishment

3. Responsible for cost control programs in the areas of payroll, food, beverages, supplies, and utilities, so that maximum quality is obtained at minimum cost

4. Coordinates bar service for functions

5. Supervises and motivates employees

6. Inspects bar and lounge operations regularly for cleanliness and proper functioning of equipment

7. Resolves customer relations problems when brought to his or her attention

8. Assists, as needed, in all capacities, and handles guests' complaints

9. Schedules bar and lounge employees to ensure high-quality service while containing payroll costs within an established percentage range

10. Responsible for hiring and terminating employees, processing time cards, evaluating employees, and conducting training sessions, as necessary

11. Responsible for safety and security systems at the bar

12. Responsible for sanitation in all areas

13. Auditions and contracts appropriate entertainment (with the approval of the owner)

14. Responsible for taking inventories and calculating bar cost percentages

15. Responsible for maximizing food and beverage sales through proper pricing and effective advertising and sales promotional efforts

Actio n **G**uidelin es

✓ Prepare job descriptions for the various jobs to be staffed in your establishment.

✓ Design an appropriate form to be used for weekly payroll analysis.

✓ Develop a personnel manual to be given to new employees.

✓ Outline a checklist of questions to be used as an interview guide.

✓ Obtain guidelines for employment application forms and interviews from the Department of Labor.

10

FINANCIAL CONTROL OF THE BUSINESS

You can do a great job of promoting your business, packing the house night after night, and pleasing your guests, but if you don't have an effective system of financial controls, you may not earn the profits that you expected, or might incur a loss.

Two financial statements that are commonly used tools for controlling a business are the *income statement* (also known as the profit and loss statement) and the *balance sheet*. The income statement reports what you earned or lost. The balance sheet reports what you own, owe, and are worth.

A balance sheet is like a candid snapshot of your business, capturing an instance in time. In contrast, the income statement is like a movie—it has a beginning, an ending (which is your profit or loss), and a middle, which explains what happened along the way. It is critical for a businessperson to understand these two statements. When you are considering corrective actions or future plans, your income statement and balance sheet will guide your decisions.

UNDERSTANDING THE INCOME STATEMENT

In their simplest form, all income statements cover four basic areas of information: revenues, costs, expenses, and profits. Put another way, they tell you how much money you took in, how much you paid out, and the difference between the two, which will be a net gain or loss. For example,

Total Revenues	$910,000
Less: Costs	266,084
Expenses	542,360
Net Profit before Federal Income Tax	$101,556

The scant version has some value, but is very limited in its ability to point out problems and suggest improvements. Only when an income statement is fleshed out with details and percentages, as shown in Figure 10.1, can management use it as an analytical tool.

What Your Income Statement Tells You

Beyond the numbers, an income statement can show relationships between categories, such as net profit to sales, and costs and expenses to sales. These relationships are expressed as percentages. When compared with an income statement for a previous period, it can reflect progress or decline. It also can raise a number of questions about a business, such as:

- Is the business undergoing unintended changes? Is it selling more liquor than food, or more food than liquor?
- Have product costs in relation to sales gotten out of line?
- Are the various categories of expenses excessive when compared to industry standards for comparable businesses?
- Is the business generating an acceptable level of income?
- Are any trends emerging?

These questions will lead to other questions that systematically isolate problems and suggest solutions. For example, if product costs (as a

FIGURE 10.1 *Sample Income Statement*

INCOME STATEMENT FOR THE WEST COAST BAR & GRILL
for the period of January 1 through December 31, 20___

			Percent
Sales			
Food Sales	$473,200		52.0%
Beverage Sales	436,800		48.0
Total Sales		$910,000	100.0%
Cost of Sales			
Food Cost	$165,620		35.0%
Beverage Cost	100,464		23.0
Total Cost of Sales		266,084	29.2
Gross Profit from Operations		$643,916	70.8%
Controllable Expenses			
Payroll	$240,240		26.4%
Employee Benefits	36,400		4.0
Direct Operating Expenses	51,870		5.7
Advertising and Promotion	26,390		2.9
Music and Entertainment	18,200		2.0
Utilities	29,120		3.2
Admin. and General Expenses	36,400		4.0
Repairs and Maintenance	18,200		2.0
Total Controllable Expenses		456,820	50.2
Profit before Occupancy Costs		$187,096	20.9%
Occupancy Costs			
Rent (Triple Net Lease)	$46,410		5.1%
Property Taxes	5,460		0.6
Other Taxes	1,820		0.2
Property Insurance	9,100		1.0
Total Occupancy Costs		62,790	6.9
Profit before Interest and Depreciation		$124,306	14.0%
Interest		$ 4,550	0.5%
Depreciation		18,200	2.0
NET PROFIT		$101,556	11.2%

percentage of sales) have gotten out of line, management must find out why. That raises a set of questions: Is it due to carelessness and waste, lack of training, poor purchasing practices, inadequate pricing of drinks, or pilferage? Management must then look at each of those specific areas in detail, and locate the reason for the high product costs. At that point, the corrective action associated with the problem will become apparent.

UNDERSTANDING THE BALANCE SHEET

A balance sheet is a statement of what you own and owe to others, as well as a declaration of what your business interest is worth. A sample balance sheet for illustrative purposes is in Figure 10.2.

ANALYZING STATEMENTS

There are numerous accounting tools for analysis. Many of them are better left to accountants, but 11 of them in particular are useful to bar owners and managers. They measure the health of a business, signal problems that need attention, and point out strengths and weaknesses. These are:

- Pouring Cost Percentage (PC)
- Food Cost Percentage
- Labor Cost Percentage
- Expense Percentage
- Net Profit on Sales
- Rate of Return on Investment
- Current Ratio
- Acid Test Ratio
- Working Capital
- Average Guest Check
- Seat Turnover Ratio

Statistical data on operating costs may be obtained from the National Restaurant Association in Chicago, IL (*www.restaurant.org*).

FIGURE 10.2 *Sample Balance Sheet*

BALANCE SHEET OF THE WEST COAST BAR & GRILL
as of December 31, 20___

ASSETS

Current Assets

Cash on Hand	$ 8,026	
Cash in Bank	57,500	
Accounts Receivable	14,800	
Food Inventory	9,208	
Beverage Inventory	13,650	
Supplies Inventory	3,500	
Marketable Securities	64,106	
Prepaid Expenses	17,500	
Total Current Assets		**$188,290**

Fixed Assets

Furniture, Fixtures & Equipment	$172,500		
Less: Depreciation Reserve	31,050	141,450	
Leasehold Improvements	130,250		
Less: Depreciation Reserve	11,350	118,900	
Total Fixed Assets			260,350
TOTAL ASSETS			**$448,640**

LIABILITIES AND NET WORTH

Current Liabilities

Accounts Payable	14,850	
Taxes Collected	15,590	
Accrued Expenses	23,200	
Current Portion of Long-term Loan Due	4,762	
Total Current Liabilities		**$ 58,402**
Long-term Loan Balance	115,000	
Less: Current Portion Due	4,762	
Total Long-term Liabilities		**$110,238**

Net Worth

Partner A—Capital Equity	175,000	
Partner B—Capital Equity	105,000	
Total Partner's Net Worth		**$280,000**
TOTAL LIABILITIES AND NET WORTH		**$448,640**

Pouring Cost Percentage (PC)

This tells you what percentage of the selling price of a drink goes to pay for the ingredients required to make it. The percentage can be calculated for one drink or for all of the liquor sold in a given period of time. Depending on style of service, sales promotional objectives, and efficiency, percentages typically range from 18 percent to 30 percent. The formula for calculating pouring cost percentage follows:

Cost of Beverage Sold ÷ Beverage Sales = Pouring Cost Percentage
Example: $100,464 ÷ $436,800 = 23%

Food Cost Percentage

This tells you what percentage of the selling price of a food item or a meal goes to pay for the ingredients required to make it. Like the pouring cost percentage, it can be calculated for a single item or for all the food sold in a given period of time. Percentages for most table service operations range from 30 percent to 40 percent, depending on style of service, sales promotional objectives, and efficiency. Food cost percentage is calculated as follows:

Cost of Food Sold ÷ Food Sales = Food Cost Percentage
Example: $165,620 ÷ $473,200 = 35%

Labor Cost Percentage

This tells you what percentage of sales goes to pay your labor costs. It gives you an indication of how efficiently you are using your workforce. If the percentage is high when compared to industry standards for similar establishments, you may be overstaffing, paying too much overtime, or not planning and supervising jobs well enough. The formula for calculating your labor cost percentage follows:

(Payroll + Employee Benefits) ÷ Total Sales = Labor Cost Percentage
Example: ($240,240 + $36,400) ÷ $910,000 = 30.4%

Expense Percentage

This indicates how well operating expenses are being controlled. There are many categories of expenses that can be abused if not supervised carefully. Linens can be used improperly, lights can be left on in empty rooms, heat may not be turned down at night, paper goods may be wasted, or advertising expenditures may not be producing results. Most expenses are controllable. The following formula may be used to determine the relationship of any expense item to total sales:

$$\text{Expense} \div \text{Total Sales} = \text{Expense Percentage}$$
$$\text{(Utilities) } \$29,120 \div \$910,000 = 3.2\%$$

Net Profit on Sales

This number is important because it summarizes the overall ability of a business to operate profitably. Some businesses take in a great deal of revenue but do a poor job of controlling costs and expenses, and consequently make very little profit. This percentage relates profits to sales. It can also be calculated on an after-tax basis, by using the net profit amount after taxes. The formula for calculating the percentage of net profit on sales follows:

$$\text{Net Profit before Taxes} \div \text{Total Sales} = \text{Percentage of Net Profit on Sales}$$
$$\$101,556 \div \$910,000 = 11.2\%$$

Rate of Return on Investment

This is a measure of how well a business is profiting when compared to the funds invested, or how well it is paying back the investors. It is a very important piece of information to consider when buying or selling a business. It is also useful when comparing alternative investment opportunities. The formula for calculating rate of return on investment follows:

$$\text{Net Profit before Taxes} \div \text{Investment} = \text{Rate of Return on Investment}$$
$$\$101,556 \div \$500,000 = 20.3\%$$

Current Ratio

This ratio is of interest to suppliers and lenders because it reflects a firm's ability to pay its bills as they come due. Only assets consumed and replenished in the ongoing conduct of a business may be used in this calculation. Those assets, called current assets, include cash, receivables, marketable securities, inventories, and prepaid expenses (such as insurance premiums paid in advance). The current ratio relates current assets to current liabilities. Current liabilities include only those obligations that are payable on a current basis, such as accounts payable, notes payable, and accrued expenses (e.g., wages payable). The formula for calculating current ratio is as follows:

$$\text{Current Assets} \div \text{Current Liabilities} = \text{Current Ratio}$$
$$\$188,290 \div \$58,402 = 3.2{:}1$$

In the above example, the firm has 3.2 times as many current assets, as it has current liabilities. A ratio of at least 2 to 1 is generally believed to provide adequate assurance that current bills can be paid in a timely manner.

Acid Test Ratio

This test is applied in instances where a business does not have the desired minimum current ratio of 2 to 1. Only certain "quick" assets may be counted in the calculation of the acid test ratio—cash and assets that can be quickly converted into cash, namely accounts receivable and marketable securities. The sum of those three quick assets is divided by current liabilities, as shown below:

$$\frac{\text{Cash} + \text{Accts. Rec.} + \text{Marketable Sec.}}{\text{Current Liabilities}} = \text{Acid Test Ratio}$$

$$\frac{\$65,526 + \$14,800 + \$64,106}{\$58,402} = 2.5{:}1$$

In the above example, the firm has 2.5 times as many quick assets as it has current liabilities. This shows it to be in excellent financial condition and very capable of paying its current obligations when due. A 1 to 1 ratio is the minimum desired for the acid test.

Working Capital

This is a measurement of the funds available to run the ongoing affairs of a business. Lack of working capital is one of the more common reasons for business failures. Some entrepreneurs spend so much of their money on buildings and equipment that they have difficulty paying bills while their business is developing a cash flow. Working capital is the difference between a firm's total of current assets and its total current liabilities, as shown in the formula below:

$$\text{Current Assets} - \text{Current Liabilities} = \text{Working Capital}$$
$$\$188,290 - \$58,402 = \$129,888$$

Average Guest Check

This calculation tells how much each guest tends to spend, on average, when he or she patronizes your establishment. A declining guest check average may indicate that the quality of your food or drinks is slipping, or that your wait staff is not practicing suggestive selling. Appetizers, desserts, and after-dinner drinks can double a guest check, but they need to be mentioned enthusiastically by wait staff. The average guest check is calculated as follows:

$$\text{Total Sales} \div \text{No. of Guests Served} = \text{Average Guest Check}$$
$$\$910,000 \div 49,500 = \$18.38$$

Seat Turnover Ratio

This is an indicator of how successfully you are drawing people to your establishment. A low or declining seat turnover ratio is of concern, because it represents an erosion of the guest base. If not corrected, the business may fail. The following formula shows how a seat turnover ratio can be calculated. You should use the actual number of days your establishment is open for business during the period being analyzed. In the following example, the 100 seats were filled 1.7 times a day on average:

$$\text{No. of Guests Annually} \div \text{No. of Seats} \div 365 \text{ days} = \text{Seat Turnover Ratio}$$
$$61{,}980 \div 100 \div 365 = 1.7 \text{ times a day}$$

TRENDS

Food and beverage cost percentages may be calculated daily, weekly, or monthly. Integrated computer systems can perform this task very easily. For those who still compute costs manually, the maximum recommended period is one month. Beyond that, results become increasingly less useful for solving problems. Some cost control systems calculate daily, weekly, and monthly percentages. Weekly and monthly percentages are more indicative of emerging trends than are a single day's percentage, because good days average out bad days. Consequently, when you have a high monthly percentage, you know you have a more serious problem. On a daily basis, numbers may be inconclusive. For example, if there was an unexpected storm one day and no one came to eat at your bar, that day's food cost percentage would be unusually high, because a lot of food was prepared but very little sold. The next day when you run out the carried over food, there would be an offsetting low food cost percentage, because you would have normal sales with virtually no new food used.

The same applies to liquor. For example, an accidentally broken bottle of whiskey can cause a glaring rise in one day's pouring cost percentage, but when viewed in the context of a whole week's business, it does not give cause for alarm. It is advisable as a matter of policy, however, to check out the reason for any drastic increase in the percentage.

Prolonged rising costs and declining patronage are of great concern to management because they may represent entrenched practices, which, if not corrected will get worse and, therefore, cannot be allowed to continue.

HOW MUCH CONTROL IS ENOUGH?

A saying in the business is, "The cost of controls should not exceed the savings they can make." In other words, do not spend dollars to chase after pennies. Every business has its own special circumstances that will dictate how much control is enough.

If an owner is actively involved in a business, a greater amount of personal control will be present. Hence, a lesser amount of formal control will be needed. As opposed to that, operations with absentee owners must have very tight controls because their profit potential and investment are at stake.

Two problems can arise, in the case of the active owner, if no controls are utilized. One is the owner may become enslaved to the business, for fear of leaving it in someone else's hands. And two, unless the owner is present every minute of every day, the business is vulnerable during any unattended periods. Controls require a little effort but can render a great deal of peace of mind and freedom. Large chain organizations have proved that with adequate controls, training, and supervision, businesses can be run very well with professional management.

A SIMPLE COST SYSTEM FOR A SMALL BAR

Some very small bars have no controls because they do not want more paperwork. For those bars, the simple control system illustrated below would be a substantial improvement. It requires only three procedures:

1. A periodic inventory
2. A record of purchases
3. A record of sales

An inventory is taken at the beginning of a period, and again at the end of the period. The duration of the period may be from one week to one month, but should not exceed a month. During the period, a record of sales and purchases is kept. At the end of the period, the following calculations are made.

Beginning Inventory, 6/1	$3,200
Plus: Purchases, 6/1–6/30	8,600
Total	$11,800
Less: Ending Inventory, 6/30	3,500
Cost of Beverage Sold	$8,300

$$\frac{\text{Cost of Beverages Sold}}{\$30,000} = \frac{\$8,300}{\$30,000} = 27.6\% \text{ Pouring Cost}$$

Unless the owner wants to work from opening to closing time every day, a minimal amount of control, such as that illustrated above, should be installed. The pouring cost percentage is a measure of the bar's efficiency. Careless pouring, giving drinks away, waste, and pilferage are all reasons why a pouring cost percentage might go up.

IDENTIFYING UNDESIRABLE PRACTICES

No matter how well management tries to screen applicants and hire good people, the possibility exists that undesirable practices may set in and result in a loss of profits and guests. Management must monitor operations carefully to deter or at least quickly discover such activities. Here are examples of unethical or illegal behaviors that directly affect your bottom line:

- Adding water to bottles to conceal shortages
- Substituting cheaper liquors for more expensive ones
- Serving drinks to other employees without charging them
- Overpouring to get bigger tips
- Giving free drinks or unauthorized discounts to friends
- Changing inventory counts to cover up for merchandise taken undetected
- Receiving kickbacks from suppliers in return for buying their merchandise and not turning them in to the management
- Accepting gifts in return for buying inferior or overpriced products
- Drinking while on duty
- Tampering with counters or meters on machines or bottles

- Faking lost guest checks, petty cash payouts, or breakage
- Leaving the cash register drawer open and not ringing up every sale

AUTOMATED BEVERAGE DISPENSING SYSTEMS

There is a wide variety of dispensing systems on the market today. Some are completely automatic, and others are little more than bottle pourers with built-in measuring devices.

The degree to which a bar will automate will depend on the size and volume of the establishment, its available funds, and its management's perception of its control problems and the bar's potential. Many reasons for installing automatic dispensing systems are put forth by their manufacturers, the most prominent being such benefits as the following:

- Mixes perfectly blended cocktails
- Dispenses drinks uniformly and consistently
- Prevents overpouring and spillage
- Eliminates pricing errors
- Ensures drinks will not be given away undetected
- Removes temptation
- Controls inventories

Though not infallible, there is no question about the capability of completely automated systems to control inventories. They also can reveal missing guest checks and cash shortages. While users regard them highly, as good as automatic dispensing systems are, they are not without their critics. The main criticisms are:

- They are costly and in some cases expensive to install.
- They are sometimes perceived as impersonal and miserly.

How the Systems Work

Each system has its proprietary differences, but in general, beverages are poured from spouts, guns, or devices attached to individual bottles.

As the system pours, the quantity of beverage dispensed is counted by a meter or a computer.

The number and types of functions a system will perform vary with cost. Some systems measure and count, while others store vast amounts of data and perform analytical calculations as well. Computerized cash registers may be integrated into the systems to provide inventory and sales reports. Examine potential savings and benefits carefully before investing in any system.

Actio*n* **G**uidelines

✓ Prepare an estimated income statement and calculate the following measurements of the health of the business:
  • Food cost percentage
  • Pouring cost percentage
  • Labor cost percentage
  • Net profit on sales

✓ Prepare an estimated balance sheet and calculate the following measurements of the financial strength of the business:
  • Working capital
  • Current ratio
  • Acid test ratio

11

MARKETING

History shows us many excellent products did not achieve their expected potential when introduced because they were not marketed properly. Occasionally, a failed or laggard product is acquired by someone who recognizes its true promise and reintroduces it with creative marketing, and before long the product becomes a hit. Similarly, the success of a bar or tavern can be enhanced with effective marketing and sales promotion.

A simple definition of marketing for a bar is to get the right products and services to the right guests, at the right time and place, and at the right price. In the hospitality field, this involves identifying clearly who your target guests are, and then satisfying their wants and needs in a way that they perceive a valued experience every time they frequent your establishment so they look forward to returning.

WHY YOU NEED A MARKETING PLAN

A marketing plan keeps your marketing activities on track. It identifies your goals and focuses the actions of all employees in a concerted effort to achieve your desired objectives. It removes guesswork and creates a stable atmosphere. When clearly communicated to all employees,

FIGURE 11.1 *Seven-Step Process for Developing a Marketing Plan*

1. Establish your overall objective
   Example: To increase sales by 40 percent next year

2. Identify your strengths and weaknesses
   Strengths   Weaknesses
   Excellent food and drinks   Lack of seating capacity
   Excellent service

3. List the alternative strategies available to you
   (i)   Add on to the existing building
   (ii) Attract more people on slow nights
   (iii) Get people to come earlier and/or stay later

4. Select the best strategy
   Assume that attracting more people on slow nights (ii) is the best strategy

5. Develop a detailed plan of action
   (i)   Conduct a survey to learn what attracts people most
   (ii) Have a different theme planned for each normally slow night
   (iii) Establish a timetable
   (iv) Hire entertainment
   (v)   Advertise and promote the events

6. Implement the plan
   (i)   Start doing it
   (ii) Keep careful records of results
   (iii) Observe the good and bad points of what you are doing
   (iv) Refine and adjust specific actions as you go along
   (v)   Reinforce the good features
   (vi) Correct the flaws

7. Evaluate the results of your efforts
   Decide whether to continue or terminate the program

it creates a team spirit that brings out the best qualities of everyone. Figure 11.1 breaks the development of a marketing plan into seven easy to understand steps.

Marketing activities encompass a broad range of tools, called the marketing mix, which includes market research, product and concept development, packaging, pricing, advertising and sales promotion, and personal selling strategies. Successful marketing programs start with an in-depth knowledge of prospective guests' wants and needs.

KNOW YOUR BUSINESS LIFE CYCLE

Most businesses pass through a life cycle, as summarized in Figure 11.2. It is essential at each stage to know where you are at, because your marketing activities should be based on what is required at each stage.

MARKET RESEARCH

The following three types of information about prospective guests can help a business plan a marketing strategy:

1. Demographic information
2. Geographic information
3. Psychographic information

FIGURE 11.2 *The Business Life Cycle*

Life Cycle Stage	Characteristics of That Stage
1. Introduction	Your business has just started. You are trying to survive and become established. Systems are being perfected.
2. Conservative Growth	A period of slow and steady growth of sales as more people learn about your establishment. You try new ideas to attract more people.
3. Rapid Growth	Your reputation spreads. The word is out that you have a unique concept and serve good food and drinks. Your popularity grows rapidly, as do your sales. Competitors notice your success.
4. Leveled Maturity	Competition intensifies as others copy your ideas, and new competitors emerge. Growth ceases and you try to hold your market share.
5. Rejuvenation or Decline	Competitors and new entrants not only take your ideas but improve on them. You must reinvent your business, again introducing new ideas that differentiate and position you ahead of the pack, or your business will decline.

In Stage 1, a business would focus its advertising on letting the public know it exists, what it offers, and where it is. In Stages 2 and 3, its advertising would change to promotions that would bring in first-time patrons and increase patronage by existing guests. In Stage 4, it would attempt to hold its market share by capitalizing on the reputation it built in the previous three stages. It would remind people about its quality and the reasons it became popular. In Stage 5, if successful in rejuvenating itself, its advertising would emphasize what is new or improved. Essentially, the whole process would start over for the new product.

Demographics are facts about people, such as their age, income, education, occupation, race, religion, and nationality. The more you know about the population in your marketing area, the better you will be able to serve them. You will be aware of their customs and special holidays—when, where, and how they spend their money, how you should price your menu, and what level of service will be expected of you.

Geographic information tells you where people live and work. It will tell you something about their dining and drinking patterns. For example, harried commuters are more apt to rush to their cars after work than are in-town dwellers.

Psychographic information deals with lifestyles and motivational influences on people's spending behavior. It can tell you such things as whether people are name-brand conscious, are influenced by peer groups, or are socially oriented and have a need to keep up with others.

It is possible to buy market information, if you can afford it. There are firms that constantly conduct market research and sell their findings to businesses. Their names are available at the reference department of your local library and in business and telephone directories.

If you cannot afford to buy data, you can gather a great deal of information on your own through observation and discreet questioning. Public information agencies, such as chambers of commerce, state and city offices, and newspapers and radio stations, can provide much information.

In addition to researching your prospective guests, check out your competition. The success of a competitor may be an indicator of how well you will do. It is also a good way to cross-fertilize your own ideas.

Study the economic trend of your community. Focus on where it is headed, not on what it was like in the past—because, as investment advisors are prone to say, past history is no guarantee of future performance. Your market research will influence decisions that may make or break you. Following is a list of questions that should be answered by your research:

- What kinds of competition are there in your proposed marketing area? What are your competitors offering? Menu? Style of service? Entertainment? Atmosphere and décor?
- How successful are your competitors?
- What kinds of guests do they attract?

- What special things are they doing to attract their clientele?
- What are their merchandising and pricing policies?
- What are their apparent strengths and weaknesses?

You cannot be sure your concept is truly unique until you research your competitors. Recognizing your competitors' strengths will stimulate your creative processes and inspire you to do your best. After examining your competitors' merchandising styles and target markets, you can devise your own marketing strategies to reach your desired clientele. By assessing the intensity of the competition, you will have some idea of the degree of difficulty you can expect in your effort to penetrate the market.

The most direct way to gather information about your competitors is to patronize their establishments. Observe carefully. Chat with wait staff. Question suppliers and delivery people. Talk to other business owners, and anyone else who might give you valuable information. Don't be bashful about your research efforts; you can be sure your competitors will be researching your business as soon as you open. Everything you learn will help you develop a competitive strategy and capitalize on their weaknesses. Below are some things to look at when researching another bar or restaurant:

- Type of bar or restaurant
- Capacity of the establishment
- Waiting time to be seated and then to be served
- Efficiency and friendliness of the host/maître d'
- Wine, liquor, and food menus
- Quality of food and drinks
- Cost in relation to quality
- Variety of offerings
- Setup of tables
- Décor of rooms
- Overall cleanliness of the facility
- Availability of wait staff when needed
- Noise level
- General ambiance of establishment
- Sales promotional techniques utilized—displays, price inducements, personal selling
- Accuracy of bill and timeliness of presentation
- Promptness in collecting your payment

IDENTIFYING YOUR TARGET MARKET

Most businesses in the public hospitality field want everyone to feel welcome in their establishment. As a result, they often make the mistake of thinking their target market is everyone, when in fact their target market is that segment of the population that strongly wants what they offer or is most apt to patronize their establishment.

Everyone does not want the same thing. People over 45 do not generally have the same tastes for music or ambiance as people in their early 20s have. Most bars and restaurants have a stronger following within certain demographic groups. The best way to identify your target market is to segment the market according to demographic, geographic, and psychographic variables, as shown in Figure 11.3.

CLARIFYING YOUR GUESTS' WANTS AND NEEDS

Supplement your own observations by researching hospitality industry trade journals. Popularity indexes of food and drink preferences are periodically published by trade journals. The National Restaurant Association also compiles data on guest spending patterns and other industry statistics, providing valuable information on the performance of eating and drinking establishments in its annual publication *Restaurant Industry Operations Report.*

FIGURE 11.3 *Sample Guest Profile*

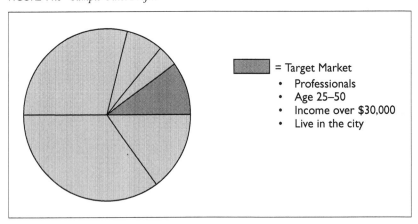

FIGURE 11.4 *Guest Analysis*

Type of Guest	Want or Need	Response
Workers, lunchtime	Nourishment	Good, healthy food
Workers, after work	Relaxation	Comfortable seating, music
Dinner guests, tourists, visitors	Excitement	Interesting food, exotic drinks
Entertainment seekers	Stimulation	Music, dancing
Social guests	Meet people	Informal setting, stand-up bars

Identify your guests' wants or needs when they come to your establishment, and identify how you can satisfy them. Many bars have two distinct types of clientele. In the daytime they cater to workers, shoppers, and tourists; at night they cater to a social, fun-seeking clientele. Careful planning will allow you to serve both groups without sacrificing your desired image. Figure 11.4 illustrates how guests' wants and needs may be analyzed.

COMPETITIVE STRATEGIES

There are three types of competitive strategies you may consider as a result of your research findings. The first is a *cost-based market penetration strategy*—that is, you can penetrate the market with lower prices than your competitors. This is a popular strategy, but it is feasible only when accompanied by tight cost controls and cost-minimization efforts in all expense areas, so you can still make a profit and survive.

If you do not have any competition, you may charge what the traffic will bear (a practice referred to as *skimming the market*) for as long as your offering is in demand, and until competitors appear. It is essential, however, to be aware of your *pricing points*. These are your limits—prices above which guests do not perceive your product or service to be worth what you are charging.

The second strategy is a *differentiation strategy*, which refers to distinguishing in your guest's mind your business from your competitors' establishments. You can differentiate your business by advertising its uniqueness or high quality. Uniqueness can take many forms. A bar's unusual atmosphere and décor, music, specialized style of service, or menu offerings can differentiate it from its competitors. You also can make your business appear to be different simply by the way you position your competitors' products in your advertising. An example of this would be the following statement in an advertisement: "PLAY SMART—NOW YOU CAN DINE AND DANCE IN A SMOKE-FREE BAR WITH A HEALTHY MENU!" If competitors still allowed smoking and offered only deep-fried, fast foods, this bar would appear different to its target market.

The third strategy is *concentration,* which is focusing on a particular guest group, geographic location, or style of service. While the cost-based and differentiation strategies are aimed at the entire potential market, the concentration strategy aims at a particular need of a specific segment of your target market.

HOW TO GET NEW GUESTS

Some guests will patronize your establishment because you are conveniently located. Others will come to your bar because it is the new place in town or because they have heard good things about it. Many, however, will intend to come to your place someday, yet will never get around to doing so unless you do something special to draw them in.

Consumers, knowingly or unknowingly, go through a decision-making process before making purchases. They pass through five stages, and the same process often applies to people who try a new bar or restaurant. The process may be depicted as follows:

1. *Awareness.* This occurs when a person first realizes you exist.
2. *Interest.* This develops when they hear something good about your place from a friend.
3. *Evaluation.* This occurs as they mull over what they have heard and decide whether or not to try it sometime.
4. *Trial.* This is when the guest visits your bar to see if he or she likes it.
5. *Adoption or rejection.* This is the result of the guest's first experience at your establishment.

The consumer's decision-making process indicates how hard it is to get regular guests, and the importance of taking good care of your present guests. They are both a source of income and valuable word-of-mouth advertising.

To get new guests, you must first make them aware of your existence through advertising and sales promotion programs and, better yet, through pleasing your present guests so they will tell their friends about your establishment. Without question, the most effective advertising a business can have is word-of-mouth advertising from satisfied guests.

THE INTERNET—A POWERFUL MARKETING TOOL

People are increasingly using the Internet as their primary source for information and businesses are finding it to be an indispensable part of their marketing activities. A bar can use the Internet to convey information about its location, entertainment schedule, special promotions, menu offerings, and hours and days of operation, as well as show through photos a sense of its ambiance—providing many reasons for people to patronize your bar.

To do this however, the Web site must be advertised; otherwise it will be like a bottle with a message in it floating in the middle of an ocean. Mention the Web site address in all media advertising, and on your menus and business cards. Try to give it an easy to remember name and link it with other highly visited Web sites.

The site should radiate professionalism, appear welcoming, and convey excitement. Unless you have significant computer savvy, it pays to have a professional Web site builder construct it.

PRICING—A MARKETING TOOL

The prices a bar charges will influence the type of clientele it attracts. Higher prices are usually associated with entertainment, a special location, or ambiance. Management should constantly challenge its prices to ensure that they are appropriate to the style of service and the quality and quantity of the products served and in line with competitors' prices for comparable offerings. At any level of pricing, the guest must perceive value commensurate with the prices they are paying.

People tend to be less forgiving of poor-quality products or services when higher prices are charged. There are few second chances given in the food and beverage business. Guests simply do not return when dissatisfied, and what is worse, they tell their friends about their poor experience.

Pricing Mixed Drinks

There are a number of ways to price drinks. Some are simple, and others are more complicated. All are acceptable as long as they cover costs and expenses, yield a desired level of profit, and are perceived by guests as being worth the value of the product they receive. Following is one method for pricing drinks:

Assume:
1. A 750 milliliter bottle of gin costs $14.50.
2. Drink prices are based on a 20 percent pouring cost. (That means 20 percent of the price of a drink goes to pay for its alcoholic ingredients.)
3. Your standard pour is 1.5 ounces. (A pour is the amount of alcohol you put into a standard drink.)
4. You allow 1.4 ounces out of every bottle for spillage. (25.4 ounces minus 1.4 ounces equals 24 salable ounces per bottle, or 16 drinks made with 1.5 ounces of alcohol each.)

Step 1. Cost of Bottle ÷ Pouring Cost % = Sales Yield
$14.50 ÷ 0.20 = $72.50 (Sales yield of bottle)

Step 2. Sales Yield ÷ No. of Drinks = Base Selling Price
$72.50 ÷ 16 = $4.53 (Base selling price of drink)

Step 3. Add a "kicker" of 50 cents to cover the cost of garnishes and mixers. Beyond that, the base price could be further adjusted to defray the cost of entertainment and other special considerations, such as the high cost of rents in premium locations and liquor liability insurance.

Using the above method, the drink in the example might sell for $5.00 to $6.50. If drinks requiring more liquors were served, the same pricing system could be used resulting in a higher selling price.

Prior to the advent of POS systems and computerized cash registers, bar owners were concerned that bartenders would not be able to remember a great many prices, and felt that mistakes would more than offset the benefits of pricing drinks individually. Consequently, a tiered pricing system was frequently used. Under the tiered system, all drinks that were made with one liquor would have one average price, all two-liquor drinks would have another, higher, average price, and so on for three-liquor drinks.

Today, POS systems and computerized cash registers can be programmed to handle as many drink prices as a bar wants to charge. Prices can vary by the type and quality of the liquors requested, for example, well liquors, call brands, and top-shelf brands. They also can vary by size of drinks, such as regular-size cocktails, doubles, and shots. Best of all, they are easy for bartenders to use—the bartender simply presses the key or image bearing the name or code of the drink. There is nothing to memorize or calculate. The register will charge the correct price and tell the bartender how much change to give the guest for a cash transaction, and integrate with a credit card reader to process a charge sale.

Pricing Wines

The philosophy for pricing wines has always been different than that of mixed drinks. This is due, in part, to the fact that wines often are sold by the bottle, and therefore command higher prices, and because they are considered add-on sales. It has always been considered best to use a flexible markup system, whereby higher cost wines are priced with a smaller percentage of markup. This method of pricing makes better wines more affordable and increases their sales. Take the following example:

Wine A costs $10.50 per bottle. It is priced with a 100 percent markup to sell at $21. The gross profit per bottle equals $10.50.

Wine B costs $32 per bottle. It is priced with a 50 percent markup to sell at $48. The gross profit per bottle equals $16.

In the above example, the establishment will earn an additional $5.50 of gross profit when they sell a bottle of wine B, even though it was marked up by only 50 percent. In addition, they will sell more better wines because many guests will recognize their greater relative value. Keep in mind: It is dollars you take to the bank, not percentages.

Pricing policies regarding wines by the glass vary widely from one establishment to another. Some bars will sell their better wines only by the bottle, because the remaining wine in an opened bottle will begin to deteriorate if not sold quickly. Other bars will charge significantly more than one-fourth of the selling price of a full bottle for a glass of wine (there are four glasses of wine in a bottle) for that same reason, and point out to patrons that buying the bottle is more economical than buying multiple glasses of the wine. Yet others limit their wine-by-the-glass choices to just a red and a white house wine, which is often a mass-marketed or bulk packaged wine that can be dispensed at lower prices.

Pricing Beer

Three main factors determine the selling price of draught (pronounced draft) beer. They are the cost of the beer, the size of the beer glass, and the size of the head poured. As with other beverages, the final selling price will be influenced by the bar cost percentage desired, and if there's a cost of entertainment or an unusually high rent. In general, however, the method for calculating the selling price of draught beer is as follows:

Assume:

Half-barrel keg costs	$75
Keg contains approx.	1,920 ounces
Cost per ounce	$0.039
Cost per 15-ounce hourglass, which actually holds about 12 ounces of beer (assuming a one-inch head is poured)	$0.468
Marked up 5 times, to accommodate a desired 20 percent bar cost percentage (selling price per glass is rounded to $2.35)	2.34

Following is an illustration of how to calculate the profit potential of a keg of beer. The actual number of glasses will depend on the type of beer keg, its contents, how the beer is drawn, and its temperature and pressure.

Again, assume a 15-ounce hourglass, which holds 12 ounces of actual beer when a one-inch head of foam is poured

Number of glasses in a half-barrel keg is 160 (1,920 divided by 12 ounces)

Price per glass	$2.35
Total sales value of a half-barrel keg (160 × $2.35)	$376
Less: Cost of half-barrel keg	$75
GROSS PROFIT	$301

In the above example, the bar is selling beer very profitably and its price is competitive. The four keys to selling a lot of beer are to

1. carry the brands your guests want;
2. keep your beer stored at the proper temperature (38°F–42°F) and gauge pressure (12–14 psi);
3. keep your dispensing system and your glasses meticulously clean; and
4. price your beers competitively.

The growing popularity of premium microbrewery beers cannot be overlooked. Many discriminating beer drinkers are willing to pay substantially more for a bottle of their favorite premium beer, provided they can take their time drinking it in a pleasant atmosphere. As with other beers, the key to selling a lot of premium beers is to know the brands your guests want and carry them. Microbrewed beers cost more at wholesale, but command a higher price at retail, and, therefore, can be very profitable.

Entertainment Surcharge

The cost of entertainment may be defrayed with a cover charge or a surcharge added to the price of drinks. Cover charges are not well accepted by guests unless the entertainment is high quality and well recognized. For that reason, a surcharge on drink prices is more commonly used. One way to calculate an entertainment surcharge is shown below. It spreads the cost of entertainment over the average number of drinks served on nights when entertainment is offered. Assume a local combo is hired at $1,425 a night:

Step 1.

$$\frac{\text{Entertainment Cost per Night}}{\text{Average No. of Drinks Sold per Night}} = \text{Entertainment Surcharge}$$

$$\frac{\$1,425}{950} = \$1.50$$

Step 2.

Base Price of Drink	$4.25
+ Entertainment Surcharge	+ $1.50
Adjusted Selling Price of Drink	$5.75

SETTING YOUR SALES GOALS

There are numerous approaches to setting sales goals, but the best is to use a combination of several methods and temper it with your own gut feeling. Industry sources, such as the National Restaurant Association's *Annual Restaurant Operations Report,* can give you typical sales figures for various types of establishments. The figures are expressed in total dollar amounts as well as sales per seat. Trade journals also conduct surveys and publish their results. These are all helpful numbers to use as cross references, but you should calculate your own numbers based on your seating capacity, expected turnovers meal-by-meal and day-by-day, and average guest check amount. There are five easy steps to follow:

Step 1. **Estimate the number of guests you might expect during each meal period, for each day of the week.**

Number of Guests Expected per Week
(Sum of daily estimates)

Lunch	395
Dinner	382
Bar Only	249
Total Guests per Week	*1,026*

Step 2. **Calculate the average menu price for each category of items on your menu.** (A weighted average method, which takes into account the popularity and sales of each item, is a more refined method, but until you are in business for a while and have a track record, this simple average method will suffice.)

Average Menu Prices

Sandwiches and Salads	$ 6.95
Entrées	14.50
Desserts	4.25
Drinks	5.50

Step 3. **Determine the amount of an average guest check by estimating what the typical guest will order.** If you expect that only one out of every two guests will order an item, you may count it fractionally. This will keep your estimate on the conservative side.

Estimated Average Guest Check per Person

Lunch	Sandwich or Salad plus Drink	$12.45
Dinner	Entrée, Salad, Dessert, plus Drink	31.20
Bar Only	Average Two Drinks	11.00

Step 4. **Multiply your average guest check by the number of guests expected per week to determine your estimated weekly sales.**

Estimated Weekly Sales

395 Guests	×	$12.45	=	$ 4,918
382 Guests	×	31.20	=	11,918

249 Guests   ×   11.00   =   2,739
Total Weekly Sales   *$19,575*

Step 5. **Finally, multiply your estimated weekly sales by 52 to arrive at your estimated annual sales.**

Estimated Annual Sales
52 weeks   × $19,575   = $1,017,900

This process tailors your sales objective to your specific business and local conditions. The resultant annual sales figure may be compared to industry averages. Figure 11.5 describes some sales tips for achieving your goals.

FIGURE 11.5   *Sales Tips*

1. *Maintain a positive attitude.* All months are not created equal. There will be slow times. You can offset slow periods to some degree by being creative and coming up with ideas that "keep smoke in the chimneys," but your main focus should be on maximizing your sales when people feel like coming out and are ready to spend money.

2. *Be prepared.* This is the secret to maximizing sales. Take advantage of the opportunities when they are there. Be ready to handle a crowd.

3. *Believe in yourself.* It has been said in fiction, "If you build it, they will come." In the public hospitality business, it can be said, "As long as you give your guests what they want, they will keep coming back." Set high standards, serve good drinks, keep your establishment clean and attractive, and offer a good value and you will soon get valuable word-of-mouth advertising from your present guests.

4. *Establish a rapport with your guests.* Let them know you care about them. That way, if you have to shut them off some night, they will not be resentful toward you.

5. *Listen to your guests.* Hear their compliments and their complaints. They are telling you what they like and don't like.

6. *Never embarrass a guest for mispronouncing the name of a wine or a menu item.* Be sympathetic and helpful. Try to build guests up, not diminish them in any way.

DON'T OVERLOOK TELEPHONE SELLING

A telephone or email sales blitz is an excellent way to notify the business community of your function rooms and group packages. Telephone calls and e-mails (with links to your Web site, where photos and extensive information can be viewed) are less costly and faster than personal visits, and if handled correctly can be just as effective. You can solicit a variety of bookings—such as retirement parties, holiday and birthday parties, promotion parties, sales meetings, and awards presentation meetings.

When telephone calls are used, carefully plan and test the message. A telephone script should contain all of the basic elements of a personal sales call, namely

- a brief introduction that tells the listener who you are and the purpose of your call;
- an attention getting statement that gives the listener a reason for continuing to listen;
- a discussion of the features and benefits of your offering;
- an opportunity for the listener to ask questions or voice any objections; and
- an appeal for an action of some sort or a subsequent meeting.

YOUR MENU IS A POWERFUL SELLING TOOL

Menus have three basic purposes. The first is to let guests know what you offer, the second is to let them know how much things cost, and the third, though somewhat less obvious purpose, is to promote the sale of certain, highly profitable, items. Sales may be enhanced by bringing certain items to the attention of guests. Boxing an item, like the example in Figure 11.6, makes it stand out on a menu.

Studies have shown that the eyes tend to follow certain patterns when reading menus, as illustrated in Figure 11.7. Knowing this, you can place items you want to promote in strategic locations.

FIGURE 11.6 *Boxed Menu Item*

El Toro

MARGARITAS
$6.95

served with
Nachos and
Jalapeño Dip

FIGURE 11.7 *How Guests Tend to See Your Menu*

MENU		
3rd spot		2nd spot
	First spot to be seen	
4th spot		Last spot

HOW A WINE LIST SELLS

Wines will sell much better if they are promoted, and your wine list is your best sales promotion tool. A good wine list should not be so long as to be confusing, but it should have enough choices to be interesting. It should provide an adequate complement to your food menu. Be sure to include the items that are popular in your area.

When designing a wine list, choose descriptive words that are easy to understand. Avoid vague expressions like "It has excellent nose and a lasting taste that challenges the palate." Also shun snobbish words that may send inappropriate messages to inexperienced wine drinkers. Try to use positive words that will enhance the appeal of your wines and assist your guests in matching them with food items. Operate on the premise that all your wines are good, it's just that some are better with certain foods. If a wine is not good, you should not carry it.

Check your wine inventory turnover periodically to weed out the slow movers; pair them with a food item on your menu or a *wine special* promotion card. It is good to search out new wines that your guests might enjoy, but do not make your bar a testing ground for every new product.

A logical order for posting wines on your wine list is 1) before-dinner wines, 2) red dinner wines, 3) white dinner wines, 4) sparkling wines, and 5) after-dinner wines. Wine lists should be printed on substantial stock so as not to quickly wear or become dog-eared. Your name should appear prominently on all wine lists. As with menus, your design can promote certain wines through boxing their names or highlighting with a special style of print or color.

WAYS TO INCREASE WINE SALES

Wait staff should be trained to present wine lists before guests order their food and to suggestively sell wines in a helpful manner. It should be noted that wine sales are truly an add-on sale, because the alternative beverage a guest is most apt to choose is water.

To make wine lists easy for guests to use, you should

- assign bin numbers to each wine, giving guests the opportunity to order by number if they cannot pronounce the name of the wine;
- use large type sizes, which make wines seem less intimidating to inexperienced wine drinkers and assists people with visual impairments;
- print wine lists on white or very light colored stock for easy reading with covers that coordinate with the décor and the mood;
- use descriptions that clearly describe a wine and suggest foods that will go well with it or vice versa;
- select a wine list size that is appropriate to your table sizes, because oversized and odd-shaped wine lists can monopolize a tabletop and be a nuisance to guests; and
- proofread wine lists carefully before approving them for printing—especially when foreign names and terms are used.

Some establishments have incentive plans to stimulate the wait staff to suggest wines to guests before they order food. Table tents and menu clip-ons can sometimes be used to promote a particular type of wine. It is a good idea to post a wine chart near the servers' pick up station at the bar (but out of guests' sight) for quick, easy reference.

THE GRAND OPENING

People are attracted to grand openings. They represent something new, perhaps a better deal. The grand opening is the most important time for a bar or restaurant to do things right. This is when you really can impress new guests and leave them bubbling with satisfaction and ready to tell their friends about the great new place they discovered. Unfortunately, many establishments waste the opportunity to cash in on their grand opening and, in some cases, it takes months to recover from an initial flurry of bad word-of-mouth advertising. To ensure a successful grand opening, you should

- not have a grand opening until you are ready to do everything right. Carefully plan a schedule of preliminary activities to ensure you will be ready on the designated date of the grand opening.
- conduct thorough training of your staff prior to the grand opening.
- test all equipment to make sure it is properly assembled, clean, and functional. Do so adequately in advance to allow tradespeople time to come back and make corrections, if necessary.
- make sure all of your licenses and permits are in place before the grand opening date. More than one opening has had to be postponed because of a last minute snag. Work closely with the licensing authorities.
- coordinate deliveries in advance with all of your suppliers to avoid distractions, shortages, or returned merchandise on the day of the grand opening.
- have a private party before going public with your grand opening. A function where you invite your relatives and close friends, business associates, and anyone who can ever do (or has done) you any good—such as media people; suppliers; politicians; liquor, fire, and health authorities; lenders and investors; and contractors. Make the event free, and expect a high rate of attendance.

This is a chance to strut your stuff in a friendly atmosphere. No one will complain if something goes wrong at this dry-run event, because the price is right, and because they are interested in seeing you succeed. Nonetheless, every detail, including mistakes and problems, should be handled as though the people were paying guests. The purpose of this function is to iron out wrinkles, and because it is your final exam, you should be thoroughly prepared.

The best planned grand opening will be of little value if people do not know about it. You must advertise and publicize it well in advance, so that people can talk it up with their friends and make plans to try your establishment. A frequently used technique for announcing your grand opening with a big splash is to have all of your contractors and suppliers sponsor a large newspaper advertisement that congratulates you on your opening and wishes you well. The contractors have made money on you and the suppliers will make a lot of money on you in the future if you are successful, so it is in their interest to help you. Besides, it places their name in the public's eye as well and also serves as an advertisement for their business. Everybody wins.

There are other things that should be done to announce a grand opening:

- Visit all nearby merchants to introduce yourself. Other businesses are frequently asked by their guests for restaurant and bar recommendations.
- Send a direct mailing to all businesses within your dominant marketing area. Include a copy of your menu and information about your hours and offerings. Be sure to emphasize your name and address prominently, so that if the recipient does not read the entire mailing, they will at least know who you are and where you are.
- Make contact with any visitor information centers in your community. Leave appropriate literature for their information racks.
- Put up an eye-catching "Coming Soon" sign in your front window announcing the date of the grand opening. This should be done well in advance to attract the attention of the most people possible.

FREE PUBLICITY

The print media welcomes newsworthy publicity releases from businesses. On slow news days, editors who have the responsibility of filling many pages with print will use press releases. Publicity articles can be about a wide variety of things, such as grand openings of new businesses, new products, a significant contribution to a charity, an award from a professional association, a change of name, or a promotion of a key person. They cannot be blatantly self-serving, contain unsubstantiated claims, or be critical of other products. In short, they cannot be advertisements. But, if they are genuinely newsworthy, well-written, and submitted on time, they stand an excellent chance of being published.

Free publicity is more valuable than paid advertising, because readers tend to believe news articles more than advertisements. Many people do not realize publicity articles are very often written by the business they describe.

Photographs make publicity articles much more interesting. They increase the readership rate dramatically and, if of good quality, editors like to run them. It is worth trading a meal and a couple of drinks to have a professional photographer take a picture for you. The quality of their prints is beyond what most people could produce, and they know how to compose a subject.

Following are some tips for writing successful publicity articles:

- Find out your local newspapers' deadlines for copy, so that you submit time-sensitive articles adequately in advance of the papers' deadline.
- Send articles to the appropriate editor. For example, an article on the sponsorship of a softball team should be sent to the sports editor, while an article announcing the appointment of a new manager should be sent to the business editor.
- Type articles on plain white paper, double-spaced; however, if you have a really important news story that can't wait, telephone the editor.
- Use the five w's when writing publicity articles. In the first paragraph, summarize the *WHO, WHAT, WHEN, WHERE, WHY,* and *HOW* of the story. Then proceed to give the details in subsequent paragraphs. If people read only the first paragraph, they will at least know your name and the important facts.

- Let the editor know that a longer article was written exclusively for his or her paper.
- Indicate that an article is "submitted for publication on a space-available basis" if it is not time sensitive. This gives it a greater chance of being published.
- Where possible, run a paid advertisement on the same page that the publicity article (and photograph) appear. You can make claims and self-serving statements in your ad. The credence given to the publicity article will tend to transfer to what is said in the paid ad, giving its claims greater acceptance.

If public speaking is your cup of tea, take advantage of opportunities to relate to the community. Many groups are constantly looking for interesting speakers and would love to have a presentation on wine and beer, or on the history of taverns. It is good way to make acquaintances, elevate the image of your establishment, and get additional publicity—speaking events usually are announced by the sponsoring group in a press release.

THE ONGOING CAMPAIGN—KEEP THEM COMING BACK

Guests enjoy being catered to. Special attention makes them feel appreciated and interested in coming back soon. There are many ways to give special attention to guests. A friendly greeting when they arrive and a thank you and good-bye when they leave, make their visit much more personal. This is especially effective when done by the owner or manager—everyone likes to know the manager.

Other sales and promotional items are table tents and lobby posters that announce future events, such as for New Year's Eve and Mother's Day or dinner/theater combination packages.

Theme nights are very successful in some bars. They give guests an opportunity to participate in the event. Figure 11.8 is a compilation of 70 ideas. Some are straightforward, such as holiday observances; others require a creative flair and the right setting. All will stimulate your creative forces and suggest other ideas not named. Consider all of the possibilities associated with themes, contests, prizes, special music, and decorations.

FIGURE 11.8 *Special Event and Theme Suggestions*

Rapper's Night	October Fest
Elvis Night	Kentucky Derby
Labor Day	Name That Tune Contest
Columbus Day	Roaring Twenties
Veteran's Day	Cabaret Night
Football Day	My Fair Lady
Thanksgiving Day	Masked Ball
Christmas Day	M*A*S*H Bash
New Year's Day	Country Fair
Super Bowl Sunday	Halloween Party
Homecoming Weekend	Marathon Mania
Olympics	Baby Picture Night
Mardi Gras	Disco Night
Hockey Games	Dance Contest
Basketball Games	Salute to the Sixties
Sidewalk Sales	Chinese New Year
St. Patrick's Day	Jamaican Style Reggae
April Fool's Day	Hawaiian Cruise
Easter	Election Day Party
Mother's Day	Down Memory Lane
Father's Day	Bahama Beach Party
Graduation Day	Old Time Movie Night
Independence Day	Aprés Ski
Cajun Night	Beatle Mania
Washington's Birthday	Comedy Night
Lincoln's Birthday	Woodstock Remembered
TGIF	Platter Party
Art Exhibit	Sadie Hawkins Night
Patriot's Day	Mystery Dinner
May Day	Chicago 1920s
Dollar Days	Soap Opera Night
Theater Night	Sing Along
Carnival Night	Fashion Show
Wine Tastings	Salute to the Armed Forces
Looney Toons Night	Stooge Fest
Baseball Night	Reality Show Night

HOW DO YOU WANT TO BE PERCEIVED?

The answer to this question will be the cornerstone of all your advertising, merchandising, sales and promotions, and publicity activities. Once you decide how you want the public to view your business, you must challenge every activity you conduct to be certain it clearly signals your desired image.

Your choice of radio stations and the tone of your commercials, the location of your advertisements in newspapers, the graphic design and typefaces used, and the hard-sell or soft-sell message of your ads all transmit an image of your business. Advertising budgets typically range from 2 percent to 3 percent of sales in the restaurant and bar business (however, some are as low as 0 percent and others as high as 5 percent).

All employees should have a clear understanding of your desired image and how best to convey it. They are at the point of contact with your guests and can do the most to reinforce your image.

WHY ADVERTISE?

Advertising has become a fact of life in the business world. People expect it, look for it, and in spite of many abuses, still place a great deal of trust in it. There are many reasons to advertise bars and restaurants, but here are 15 of the most common:

1. To introduce new entertainment
2. To announce special holiday and theme events
3. To publicize a new or changed menu
4. To position your establishment a certain way
5. To reposition your competition
6. To attract new guests
7. To test new ideas
8. To let the public know what you are doing
9. To resell lost guests
10. To introduce a new management
11. To report achievements to the public
12. To create and maintain a certain image
13. To increase sales
14. To keep your name in the public's eye, particularly if your competitors advertise
15. To engender word-of-mouth advertising

Using Advertising Media Effectively

A great deal of money is wasted on the wrong kind of advertising by businesses desperately seeking to reach new guests. Location and frequency are critical considerations when placing ads. Your ad must run in the proper newspaper or radio or television station. To reach your target market, your ad must air at the right times on the radio and be placed in the right position in the case of newspapers. For example, the inside, lower corner of a newspaper page is a poor location for an ad because many people never see that part of the pages.

The frequency of an ad is also important. The chances of a reader seeing an ad that is run one time is pure luck. If the ad is run regularly, then chances are much greater that the reader will see it. In general, it is better to run a smaller size ad more often than a larger size ad just once. This is especially true with radio advertising, where there is no opportunity to cut out and save a commercial. Figure 11.9 is a list of types of media, and some of the advantages and disadvantages of each.

A *ctio n* **G** *u i d e l i n e s*

✓ Develop a seven step marketing plan for a new bar.

✓ Describe in a detailed paragraph the identifying characteristics of your target market.

✓ Write a press release announcing the grand opening of your bar.

✓ Create a beverage menu that includes wines, beers, and spirits.

✓ Calculate the selling prices of a 5 ounce glass of table wine, a 12 ounce glass of draft beer, and a highball made with 1.5 ounces of bar whiskey.

✓ Plan an advertising campaign based on 3 percent of your estimated sales, allocating the funds among the media you select.

✓ Make a list of the people you would invite to your preopening party.

FIGURE 11.9 *Media Analysis*

NEWSPAPERS

Advantages
- Timely, contain news of the day
- Easy to change on short notice
- Published frequently
- Can tie-in advertisements with local events
- Less expensive than magazines and broadcast media

Disadvantages
- Short life, usually discarded daily
- Ads may get buried among many others
- Some people read certain sections only
- Papers are not as well read on certain days
- Newsprint is not well suited for high-quality photos

MAGAZINES

Advantages
- Have a long life, may be saved
- May have multiple readers, are shared, and reread
- May lend prestige to advertiser
- Can be highly targeted to demographic groups, geographic areas, particular lifestyles, and special interests
- Better quality paper allows for high-quality photos

Disadvantages
- Require long lead times up to several months
- May be expensive
- Advertiser may pay for wasted circulation attracted by subscription premiums, rather than real interest

BILLBOARDS

Advantages
- Good for reminder ads
- Useful for giving directions

Disadvantages
- Not allowed in certain locations
- Can only accommodate short messages
- Viewership limited mainly to motorists

CAR CARDS

Advantages
- Most effective in mass transportation vehicles
- Can be located very precisely

Disadvantages
- Viewership limited to riders
- Most useful for short messages or reminder ads

FIGURE 11.9 *Media Analysis (Continued)*

HANDBILLS

Advantages
- Recipient can be targeted easily
- Relatively inexpensive
- May contain coupons and be saved

Disadvantages
- May create backlash, if they cause littering
- Considered junk mail by some people
- Must be very catchy or they are thrown away

DIRECT MAIL

Advantages
- Can be personalized
- Highly selective; good targeting is possible
- Can be saved or passed on to others
- Computerized mailing lists available
- Can include coupons

Disadvantages
- Very expensive
- Often thrown out as junk mail
- Low percentage of return, usually under 5 percent

RADIO

Advantages
- Easy to target market through choice of station
- Captive audience during drive times
- 99 percent of homes are said to have radios
- Over 95 percent of all cars are said to have radios

Disadvantages
- Audio only; can't save or cut out
- Lacks visual appeal

TELEVISION

Advantages
- Has both audio and visual appeal
- Easy to target market through choice of program
- Usually no extra charge if commercial is produced by the TV station
- Can be heard from another room without viewing

Disadvantages
- Longer time required to produce commercial
- Relatively high cost if commercial is produced by an advertising agency
- Can't be saved (unless taped)
- Remotes allow muting out of commercials
- TIVOs and VCRs allow fast-forwarding through commercials

12

KNOW YOUR PRODUCTS

The origin of alcoholic beverages as a potion that made one feel better or helped cure maladies is lost in the distant past, along with the bones of the first ancient shepherd who might have tasted a handful of fermented wild grape juice and unwittingly discovered wine. Today, we can only speculate on how or when alcoholic beverages were discovered, but we do know that ever since then they have been refined and developed by every stage of civilization, to the point where we now have an alcoholic beverage for every palate, food, occasion, and pocketbook.

In the course of starting and operating an alcoholic beverage establishment, you will need to buy an initial inventory of wine, beer, and spirits that will satisfy your clientele. You will also need to replenish that supply weekly. Beyond that, you often will be asked to recommend a wine to a guest, or to suggest an appropriate substitution for an item that you do not carry. You may also wish to offer wine tastings in your establishment. As a professional in the hospitality field, you on occasion may be invited to speak to a club on wine or liquors.

To do these things, you must have at least a working knowledge of the many products available. You should be able to discern their differences and be able to discuss them confidently. This chapter will provide you with the basic information on wine, beer, spirits, and liqueurs that will allow you to do that.

WINES

There are five general types of wines. Because wine is usually consumed with a meal, the wines in Figure 12.1 are broken down as they relate to the various parts of a meal.

Which Wine with Which Food

Most people believe the flavors of red dinner wines complement the flavor of red meats, particularly steaks and roast beef. White dinner wines are usually found to go best with light meats, such as veal, fish, and fowl, because the clean, light taste of white wine does not overpower the delicate flavors of those meats. Rosés, Champagnes, and other sparkling wines go well with all types of food, and are excellent as appetizer and dessert wines as well.

Always be guided by the principle that guests are entitled to their own preferences. To assist guests that appear to need help in ordering wine, a skilled server might introduce the wine list with a comment, such as, "We have some very nice red wines that go well with our red

FIGURE 12.1 *Wine Types*

Type of Wine	Examples
1. Appetizer Wines	Dry Sherry, Vermouth
2. Dinner Wines	
Red	Burgundy, Chianti, Cabernet Sauvignon, Beaujolais
White	Chablis, Chardonnay, Liebfraumilch, Pouilly Fuissé
3. Dessert Wines	Port, Cream Sherry, Muscatel
4. Sparkling Wines	Champagne, Asti Spumanti, Sparkling Burgundy
5. Blush and Rosé Wines	White Zinfandel, Rosé

meat entrées and some delightful white wines that complement light meats." After that, it's the guest's choice. Above all, be careful not to embarrass guests for their lack of knowledge about wine or their mispronunciation of a name.

Storing Wines

Only wine bottles with corks need to be stored on their sides. This prevents the cork from drying and becoming porous and brittle. Bottles with plastic or metal caps can be stored upright. The ideal temperature for a storeroom is about 60°F.

Serving Wines

Red dinner wine should be served at cool room temperature, 55° to 65°F. White wine should be refrigerated and served at about 45°F.

Premium red wine will develop a fuller aroma if opened and left to stand uncapped for about 45 minutes before serving. This is not practical to do in busy bars, but it is possible in banquet wine service. Some wine experts contend that merely uncorking the bottle does little to develop the wine, citing that the most effective way to achieve the desired result is to decant wines.

How to Open Wine Bottles

- *Champagne.* Tilt the bottle, and while grasping the cork firmly with one hand, slowly turn the bottle with your other hand. The cork will start to come out very slightly after three or four turns. After a few more turns it will come out completely without the champagne gushing.
- *Corked still wines.* Insert the auger of a corkscrew straight into the middle of the cork, as far down as it will go, then pull the cork out slowly and steadily. Smell the cork to be sure it has not become pungent, and check the cork for damage.

FIGURE 12.2   *Master Riddler, Ramon Viera, Performing His Skill in the Historic Schramsberg Sparkling Wine Aging Caves*

Photo courtesy of Schramsberg Vineyards, Calistoga, CA

How Much Wine to Serve

Appetizer and dessert wines have a greater alcoholic content than do dinner and sparkling wines, therefore, smaller portions of those wines are served. Three ounces is generally considered adequate.

Dinner wines are considered part of a meal, because they are consumed with food. Four to 5 ounces (depending on the glass size) is considered an appropriate portion.

Sparkling wines, if served with food, are treated like dinner wines (4 to 5 ounces), but if served before or after the meal, they are treated like appetizer or dessert wines (3 ounces).

How to Judge Wine

There are several instances when a bar manager will need to know how to judge wines—when buying them, when a guest complains about a wine not being good, and when conducting wine tastings. Figure 12.3 breaks down the steps for how to best taste wine.

FIGURE 12.3 *How to Taste Wine*

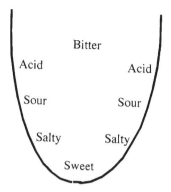

The tongue can sense five tastes:
sweet, salty, sour, acidic, and bitter

The taste buds of the tongue transition from one zone to another,
but are most distinguishable in the areas shown.

HOW TO TASTE WINE

1. Sip a small amount of wine
2. Roll it around in your mouth
3. Suck a small amount of air into your mouth
4. Roll the wine around in your mouth again
5. Focus your attention on the various sections of your tongue to isolate particular qualities of the wine
6. Swallow the wine
7. Focus on the aftertaste

Three factors are most often used to evaluate wines:

1. *Color.* The color of a wine should be clear and shiny, regardless of whether it is a red or white wine. Any wine that appears dull or cloudy is inferior. The color of a wine may be checked by viewing it through a glass held up to a light.

2. *Aroma.* The aroma of a good wine should be pleasing, not overwhelming, and never pungent. It should be faint, yet noticeable enough to be exciting.

3. *Taste.* Finally, the taste should be engaging to the palate. Some wines are intended to be sweet, and others dry. Sweet and dry are relative terms, with dry referring to the lack of sweetness.

A good wine should always have a satisfying taste, given its own characteristics. Signs of poor wines are vinegar-like flavors, an unclear appearance, and a strong or unpleasant aroma.

How Wines Are Named

Some wines are named after the region where they are produced. These are called *generic* names. Some examples of generically named wines are Burgundy, Rhine, Bordeaux, and Concord. Other wines are named after the variety of the principal grape from which they are made. Those are called *varietal* names. Examples of varietal names are Cabernet Sauvignon, Pinot Noir, Chardonnay, and Catawba.

The choice of a name is usually decided by the relative popularity of each option. If the region is more highly acclaimed, that is the name the producer will most likely choose. If the grape variety is the most prestigious, that is what the producer will use. Wines also may be given proprietary names if they would have greater market value. An example of a proprietary wine is Francis Coppola Rosso, a still, red wine produced by the vineyards of movie producer and winery owner, Francis Ford Coppola. There are controls associated with the production of wines bearing certain names. To be able to use those names, wineries must adhere to strict regulations.

Wine Tastings

The most common way to taste wine is to begin with the white wines, starting with the lighter, dryer ones and proceeding to the sweeter and fruitier ones, followed by the red wines, again starting with the lighter, dryer ones and moving on to the full-bodied, sweeter ones.

Another way to taste wine, when judging it for purchasing consideration, is the *blind tasting.* In a blind tasting session, all the wines are wrapped in paper bags with just the bottle necks exposed for pouring. In this way, the tasters are not influenced by label information and brand names, and must rely solely on their sensory perception of the taste, color, and aroma. This type of tasting is best suited to tasting a group of similar wines—cabernet sauvignons, for example.

How to Read a Wine Label

Information on a label can be very helpful when selecting wines. To better understand a wine, the following list of items should be checked:

- The name of the wine—varietal or generic
- The country or place of origin
- The type of grape from which it is made
- The size of the bottle
- The percentage of alcohol content
- The vintage date, if applicable
- The shipper's or importer's name, if it is an imported wine
- Any official statements that guarantee the authenticity of the wine

BEER AND ALE

Beer has been enjoyed by mankind for thousands of years. References to beer were found inscribed on Babylonian tablets that were more than 6,000 years old. Beer also played an important role in the societies of the ancient Greeks, Romans, and Hebrews, as well as the Teutonic tribes of Europe. The diary of one pilgrim reveals that beer came to America on the *Mayflower*. Whatever its origin was in the New World, it has since become a top-selling alcoholic beverage.

Types of Beers and Ale

For many years, Americans focused mainly on two malt beverages: lager beer and ale. Today, however, with the new interest in boutique or microbrewed beers and ales, there is a realization that there are numerous types of beer and ale, each with its own characteristics and special appeal.

We now have "flavored beers," with tastes that hint of banana, clove, and strawberry, among others. Following is a list of terms that apply to the more common beers and ales:

- *Beer.* An alcoholic beverage obtained by the fermentation of a malted grain to which hops have been added for seasoning.
- *Lager beer.* Any beer made by the bottom-fermentation method, and that is stored under refrigeration for maturing and clarification. Most American beers are lager beers.
- *Bock beer.* A strong beer that is heavy, dark, and rich; produced by the bottom-fermentation method. It is often prepared for consumption in spring.
- *Ale.* A pale, straw-colored beverage, made with a top-fermenting yeast that gives it a distinctive taste with a pronounced hop character and a more tart taste than beer.
- *Porter.* Made like ale by the top-fermentation method; heavier and darker than ale, but lighter than stout; less hop flavor and sweeter in taste.
- *Stout.* An extra dark brew made by the top-fermentation method; has a strong malt flavor, is made like ale and porter, but heavier than porter.
- *Malt liquor.* Made like beer, but has a fruity and spicy flavor and a higher alcoholic content than regular beer.
- *Dark beer.* Made like regular lager beer, but has a dark color (obtained from a darker toasted malt); not as sweet as bock beer.
- *Pilsner.* Inspired by the original brew from the town of Pilsen in Czechoslovakia. Refers to any conventional, golden colored, dry beer made by the bottom-fermentation method. Has a light, hoppy flavor.

Rules for Proper Beer Handling

Beer drinkers expect a good beer every time they order. It is not difficult to serve good beer, provided the dispensing equipment is kept clean and in good operating condition and the beer is handled properly. Following are a few simple rules, which if adhered to will allow you to serve a good beer every time:

- Keep beer fresh. Whenever new beer arrives, pull the older beer out to the front and place the new beer in the rear. This ensures the older stock will get used first.
- Store bottled and canned beer in a cool, dark, and dry place.
- Avoid exposing beer to freezing temperatures.
- Store kegged beer at 38°F. This allows it to be served at about 40°F in a glass. Chilled mugs or glasses are always desirable.
- Serve beer in clean glasses; any residual soap or oily film on glasses causes beer to go flat.
- Put keg beer into refrigeration immediately after delivery.

Bartenders should be trained to solve beer problems. If regular maintenance is performed on equipment, and the dispensing system is cleaned on a regular schedule, there should be a minimum of problems related to beer. Nevertheless, bartenders should be acquainted with the information in Figure 12.4 that presents potential problems in beer.

FIGURE 12.4 *Potential Problems in Beer*

Problem	Possible Cause
Flat Beer	• Greasy glasses • CO_2 pressure not turned on
Loose Foam	• Drawing too short a head • Not drawing beer properly • Flat beer causes (see above)
Cloudy Beer	• Bottled or canned beer was kept too warm at some time or other • Beer is old • Tap lines are dirty; need flushing
Wild Beer	• Improper drawing of beer • Beer kept too warm in package or in tap lines • Creeping pressure gauges (increasing pressure)
Off-tasting Beer	• Glasses not clean • Lines not clean • Beer too warm
Sour Beer	• Quite possible the keg was not kept properly refrigerated. The temperature of keg beer should never be allowed to rise over 50°F.

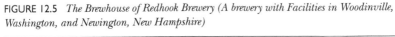

FIGURE 12.5 *The Brewhouse of Redhook Brewery (A brewery with Facilities in Woodinville, Washington, and Newington, New Hampshire)*

Photo courtesy of Redhook Brewery

The Craft Beer Industry

The craft beer industry includes four distinct markets—brewpubs, microbreweries, regional specialty brewers, and contract brewers. Though crafted beers and ales represent only about 4 percent of all beers and ales produced in the United States, they outpace the sales of all imported beers and ales, and are claimed to be the fastest growing segment of the brewing industry.

Brewpubs and Microbreweries

A brewpub is a broad term used to describe establishments that make and sell beer for consumption on the premises. Some purists say a true brewpub just makes and sells beer, nothing else. Consequently, new terms are emerging that more precisely describe the nature of establishments that make their own beer but also engage in other activities, namely restaurant breweries and brewery inns.

A microbrewery is generally considered to be a small brewery with proprietary recipes and an annual production of not more than 15,000 barrels of beer. They make small batches of specialized beers that are marketed through regular channels of distribution, and with names like Smuttynose, they capture the imagination and strike the fancy of true beer drinkers. Each brand has its small but loyal following.

DISTILLED SPIRITS

A spirit is an alcoholic beverage that is derived from the distillation of a fermented mash of grain or wine. Some distilled spirits are aged in wood to develop their body and flavor, while others are bottled immediately. Unlike wines, spirits do not continue to improve after they have been bottled.

Although the basic principle of distillation has not changed since an Arabic alchemist is said to have discovered it in the 11th century, a great many differences in liquors have emerged over the years with varying the ingredients and the production and aging techniques. The main categories of distilled spirits and the products from which they are derived are shown in Figure 12.6.

Each category of distilled spirits has subdivisions that vary according to taste and age. Whiskey, for example, includes Scotch, Bourbon, Irish, Canadian, Tennessee, Corn, Rye, and blended whiskeys. The name whiskey (spelled whisky in Scotland and Canada) stems from the Celtic name for a distilled spirit, uisgebaugh. Although the art of distilling was discovered many centuries ago, spirits of the quality we know today are much more recent.

The most common grains used in the production of spirits are wheat, corn, rye, and barley; but any fermentable food product can be distilled to produce a spirituous beverage. When a spirit is distilled to 190 proof or more, it is called a *neutral spirit,* because it has lost virtually all characteristic color, flavor, and aroma reminiscent of the product from which it was made.

When the Prohibition era ended in 1933, the federal government developed specific definitions for every type of liquor. The definitions

FIGURE 12.6 *Distilled Spirits*

Type of Spirit	Distinctive Ingredient from Which It Is Made
Whiskey	Grains: wheat, corn, rye, barley
Brandy	Distilled wine
Gin	Neutral grain spirits (flavored with Juniper berries and other herbs and spices)
Vodka	Neutral grain spirits
Tequila	Juice of the heart of the mescal plant
Rum	Sugarcane molasses

specify the ingredients that must be used, both the type and proportion, and the percentage of alcohol at the time of distilling and at the time of bottling.

Federal laws govern the names and claims that can be given to alcoholic beverages. Rye whiskey, for example, must have at least 51 percent rye in its mash. Bourbon must be produced from a mash of at least 51 percent corn. whiskeys cannot be identified as Bourbon or rye if they are distilled at over 160 proof.

Relationship of Proof to Percentage of Alcohol

Proof is a term given to the measurement of alcohol in a distillate. The term is said to have come from the days when whiskey makers would test the readiness of their liquor by pouring some on a small amount of gun powder and lighting it. If it did not burn, it was said to be underproof (not ready yet) because it did not contain enough alcohol. If it ignited with a flash, it was said to be overproof (containing too much alcohol) and needed to be watered down to a drinkable state and aged more. Finally, if it burned with a steady glow, it was considered to be just right, and had "proved" it was fit to drink.

The relationship of *proof* to *percentage of alcohol* is two to one. Put another way, percentage is one-half of proof. A 100 proof whiskey, would therefore contain 50 percent alcohol, just as a liquor with 40 percent alcohol would be 80 proof.

Bottled in Bond

If a distilled spirit meets certain government requirements, it may be stamped *bottled in bond*. The stamp is not a guarantee of quality, it merely ensures that the product conforms to certain U.S. Treasury Department requirements.

The requirements for whiskey state that it must be a straight whiskey, at least four years old, distilled at one plant, bottled at 100 proof, and secured in a U.S. Treasury Department–supervised warehouse. Other distilled spirits may also be stamped bottled in bond provided they meet specific U.S. Treasury Department requirements. The bottled in bond stamp has less significance today, because straight whiskeys are usually aged in bonded warehouses for well over four years.

Common Spirits

Straight whiskeys versus blended whiskeys. A straight whiskey is one that has been distilled at not over 160 proof, from a fermented mash of a least 51 percent of the grain for which it is named (rye or corn), and has been aged in charred, new oak barrels for at least two years.

A blended whiskey must contain at least 20 percent of a straight whiskey. The remainder may be neutral grain spirits and/or other whiskeys selected for their blending qualities. In addition, up to 2.5 percent special blending materials, such as sherry blending wine, may be included.

Canadian whiskey. By law, this must be a blend of whiskeys that has been distilled in Canada from cereal grains (corn is preferred because of its high starch content and ease of sugar conversion; however, rye, wheat, and barley malt are also used). It must be aged at least two years, though most Canadian whiskeys are actually aged six or more years. If any are aged fewer than four years, they must be so described on the label. Canadian whiskey is marketed at 80 to 100 proof levels.

Scotch whiskey. Two things in particular give Scotch whiskey its characteristic flavor: 1) the influence of the smoke from the peat moss fires used in malting the barley grains, and 2) the very clear tasting waters found in the Scottish Highlands. By international agreement, Scotch whiskey must be distilled in Scotland (but it may be bottled in any country). It must be aged for at least three years.

Scotch whiskeys may be single-malt whiskeys or blended whiskeys. Single-malt whiskeys must be produced from a single barley malt at a single distillery. Blended whiskeys may be mixtures of as many as 30 different malt and grain whiskeys. The vast majority of Scotch whiskeys are blended.

A significant amount of barreled Scotch whiskey is exported in barrels to the United States at high proofs. Upon arrival, its proof is reduced through the addition of water and it is bottled for sale under a domestic label. This is done for tax-saving reasons, because taxes on imported spirits are based on the "proof gallon." Most Scotch whiskeys are reduced to 80 to 86 proof in the United States.

Scotch whiskeys that are bottled in Scotland command higher prices than do those bottled in the United States. Part of the higher prices can be attributed to greater shipping costs. Distillers in Scotland further justify the higher prices with the contention that the waters from the Highland rivers and streams give their Scotch whiskey a special character that cannot be duplicated anywhere else.

Irish whiskey. Most Irish whiskeys are blended grain whiskeys. They are produced much like Scotch whiskeys, except that in the malting process smoke is not allowed contact with the sprouted barley as it dries. This gives the final product a different taste than Scotch whiskey. Another difference is that Irish whiskey is distilled three times. This contributes to a noticeable smoothness to the product. It is usually marketed at 80 proof in the United States.

Bourbon whiskey. Bourbon whiskey was named after Bourbon County, Kentucky, and Kentuckians take immense pride in its waters, which run through the great limestone shelf underlying their state as well as Tennessee and Indiana. The limestone imparts a distinctive quality to the waters.

America's popular contribution to the world of spirits enjoys an international reputation. Bourbon is produced at 160 proof or less, from a fermented mash of at least 51 percent corn, and is stored at not more than 125 proof in new, charred, oak barrels.

Two yeasting processes are used in the production of American whiskeys—the *sweet mash* process and the *sour mash* process. Sweet mash is produced by adding freshly cultured yeast to the mash during the fermentation stage. Sour mash is produced by adding a portion of the previous fermentation to the new mash, along with a new yeast. Bourbon is made by the sour mash process and is bottled at 80 to over 100 proof.

Tennessee whiskey. In spite of its similarities with the Bourbon production process, Tennessee whiskey has its own distinctive taste and reputation.

An important step in the production of some Tennessee whiskeys, credited for its unique flavor, is filtering it through vats of ground and tightly compacted charcoal, up to 12 feet deep.

The charcoal comes from local hard maple trees cut after the sap runs and is then burned under control at the distillery. It takes ten or more days for the distillate to completely pass through the bed of charcoal. The filtering process, which immediately follows distillation, enhances the whiskey's flavor. Tennessee whiskey is often referred to as a sipping whiskey, and is bottled at 80 to more than 100 proof.

Gin. Today, two basic categories of gin are produced—Hollands gin and dry gin. The two have extremely different tastes. Hollands gin has a flavor reminiscent of whiskey, due to the lower proof at which it is distilled. It is not very popular in the United States. Dry gin is by far the most popular. It is made from neutral grain spirits that have no characteristic grain flavor of their own, but are flavored by botanical additives.

Dry gin is a clear beverage, usually bottled at 80 to 95 proof. Because it does not require aging, it is usually bottled shortly after production. If it is to be held in storage for a while, it is kept in glass-lined containers where it cannot acquire a woody taste. Dry gins produced in the British Isles tend to be of slightly lower proof.

Fruit-flavored gins (such as lime, orange, and lemon) maintain a small market in the United States. These products have distinctive tastes and cannot be used as substitutes for regular gin. They must be clearly labeled as to their flavor.

Vodka. Vodka is defined as a neutral spirit without character, taste, or aroma. However, a growing number of flavored vodkas have appeared on the market in recent years. They have delightful qualities of their own, but generally cannot be used as substitutes in drink recipes that call for regular vodka. In the past decade, vodka has enjoyed the fastest growing sales of any distilled spirit in the United States. It is an ideal accompaniment for liqueurs, juices, soft drinks, and milk or cream products in mixed drinks.

Grain is the most commonly used product for making vodka, but it may be produced from a variety of fermentable sources, including potatoes. Most vodkas marketed in the United States are bottled in the 80 to 100 proof range.

Rum. Rum is an alcoholic distillate obtained from the fermented juice of sugarcane or its molasses. The first commercial rum in the colonies was distilled in Massachusetts in 1670 with molasses imported from the West Indies.

Today, the most common distinctions among rums in the American marketplace include white or light rum, golden or medium rum, and dark or heavy rum. So-called white rums are colorless and have gained popularity as ingredients in mixed drinks because they have a dry, light taste with only a slight suggestion of molasses. Medium rums have a golden color resulting from their longer aging in oak barrels and the addition of a small amount of caramel. Dark rums are distilled at lower proofs and as a result have a heavy concentration of congeners, which give them a full bodied taste of molasses. The mahogany color of dark rum is acquired by the addition of caramel. Most rums are bottled at 80 proof, but some rums are bottled at as high as 151 proof.

Tequila. Tequila is Mexico's famous spirit. Its origins extend as far back as the pre-Columbian culture of the Aztec Indians. It is a distillate derived from the juice of the mescal plant, which is a species of the agave plant.

Most tequila is bottled immediately in Mexico, because it does not require aging. However, a small amount of golden tequila is aged. Most tequilas are marketed at 80 proof in the United States.

Brandy. The development of brandy is said to have occurred accidentally. An enterprising Flemish ship master, seeking to increase the amount of wine he could carry on his vessel, concentrated his wines by evaporating them, with the intention of adding water back to the wine at its destination point. As it turned out, the concentrated product was received with such enthusiasm when it was tasted on arrival that no effort was made to add the water back. The new product was called by its Dutch name, *brandewijn,* which means burnt wine. The name gradually evolved to the shorter, anglicized *brandy.*

Brandy is the distillate of wine. Because wines can be fermented from a wide variety of fruits, brandies can be distilled from many kinds of wine. The most popular brandy in the world is France's cognac. However, a number of other countries produce fine brandies.

It should be noted that all cognacs are brandies, but very few brandies are cognacs. Only those brandies produced according to strict legal regulations, within the departments of Charente and Charente-Maritime in southern France, may be called cognac. The town of Cognac is located within that region and gives these brandies their famous name.

All cognacs are blended. The exceptional ones are not blended until later, but others may be blended as early as the first year. Today, most cognacs are given one of two broad classifications:

1. *3 Star.* More than 80 percent of them are aged three to five years before bottling.
2. *V.S.O.P.* Means *Very Superior Old Pale.* These cognacs are aged an average of seven to ten years.

The uniform coloring of cognac is achieved by the addition of caramel. Before bottling, cognac is brought down to 80 to 86 proof by the addition of distilled water. In order to allow the cognac time to marry its blends and additives, bottling is not done for many months after.

Cognac continues to improve in oak casks for many years, but once it is bottled, the enhancement process ceases. It has long been said, the best age for cognac is 20 to 40 years, but today very few cognacs reach that age. The high cost of keeping them in inventory and the significant loss that occurs over time through evaporation in the cask make lengthy aging uneconomical.

Brandies. Most of the brandy production in the United States is located in California, where the Thompson Seedless grape is the main species used to make brandy. American brandies should not be compared to cognac—they are quite different products. But, if evaluated on their own merits, and in terms of the markets for which they are produced, most fare quite well.

Fruit brandies. The fermented mash of fruits and berries may be distilled to make fruit brandies. Following is a list of some of the better-known fruit brandies and their sources:

- Applejack—Apples
- Calvados—Apples
- Apricot Brandy—Apricots
- Blackberry Brandy—Blackberries
- Kirsch—Cherry
- Elderberry Brandy—Elderberries
- Framboise—Raspberries
- Fraise—Strawberries

Unaged fruit brandies are colorless. The golden hue of some fruit brandies is the result of aging in wood. Color is also enhanced, in some instances, by the addition of fruit juice.

Liqueurs and cordials. The words *liqueur* and *cordial* are used interchangeably. The base spirits for virtually all liqueurs are neutral grain spirits or brandy. To this base, the flavoring materials are added. Figure 12.7 describes the flavoring of a wide variety of liqueurs.

FIGURE 12.7 *Liqueur Flavors*

Liqueur	Flavor
Advocaat	Eggnog
Amaretto	Almond
Amer Picon	Bitter orange
Anisette	Anise, licorice
Apple Jack	Apple
B & B	Mixture of brandy & benedictine
Benedictine	Cognac base, unique concoction of flavoring agents
Chambord	Raspberry
Chartreuse	Unique concoction of flavoring agents
Cherry Heering	Cherry
Cointreau	Bitter orange
Creme de Almond (Noyaux)	Bitter almond
Creme de Ananas	Pineapple
Creme de Bananas	Banana
Creme de Cacao	Chocolate, vanilla
Creme de Cassis	Black currants
Creme de Framboise	Raspberry
Creme de Menthe	Mint leaves
Creme de Vanilla	Vanilla
Creme de Yvette	Violets
Curacao	Bitter orange
Drambuie	Honey & Scotch whiskey
Forbidden Fruit	Sweet, citrus
Frangelica	Hazelnut
Galliano	Licorice, vanilla, sweet citrus
Grand Marnier	Brandy, orange
Irish Mist	Honey & Irish whiskey
Kahlua	Sweet black coffee syrup
Kummel	Caraway
Midori	Honeydew melon
Ouzo	Anise, licorice
Peppermint Schnapps	Peppermint
Pernod	Anise, licorice
Peter Heering	Black Danish cherry
Pistasha	Pistachio nut
Rock & Rye	Rocky candy, rye whiskey
Sambuca	Anise, licorice
Sloe Gin	Sloeberry (blackthorn)
Southern Comfort	Peach, honey, & Bourbon
Strega	Licorice, vanilla
Tia Maria	Sweet black coffee syrup
Triple Sec	Bitter orange
Vandermint	Chocolate mint
Yukon Jack	Peach

Actio **G**uidelines

✓ Design a wine list with recommendations on which wine goes well with each menu item.

✓ Develop a list of after-dinner drinks with a description of each one.

✓ Outline the elements of a talk that would accompany a wine-tasting session.

✓ Outline the elements of a talk that would accompany a beer-tasting session.

13

RESPONSIBLE BUSINESS PRACTICES AND THE LAWS

Alcoholic beverages are consumed by nearly 70 percent of adults in America, and when done responsibly, their consumption is socially acceptable. But because of the ill effects that can result from the misuse of alcohol, sellers and servers of alcoholic beverages are required by law to conduct their business prudently. Every state and legal subdivision thereof has rules and regulations that specify how a licensed alcoholic beverage establishment must conduct its business.

A hospitality business serves its guests best when it serves them responsibly. Bar owners and employees should abide by the spirit and the letter of the liquor laws; it is in their best interest to do so. Bartenders and servers of alcoholic beverages have a responsibility to help their guests have an enjoyable time without overindulging.

KNOW THE SIGNS OF INTOXICATION

Train your servers to always look for signs of intoxication. The challenge to a server is not to shut off a person, but to monitor their drinking in such a way that they have an enjoyable time without becoming intoxicated. Some of the signs are the following:

- Lessening of inhibitions
- Exercising poor judgment
- Impairment of reaction time
- Loss of coordination

When people have a drink, they tend to relax, their inhibitions lessen. Some become talkative, while others become quiet; but all are relaxing in their own way. If they drink at a pace of not more than one ounce of pure alcohol per hour (the liver's approximate limit for metabolizing alcohol), they could drink for quite a while without becoming intoxicated.

If they drink faster, their blood alcohol content rises, and they begin to demonstrate the first noticeable effects of intoxication: poor judgment, demonstrated by such signs as talking so loud as to irritate other guests; making outbursts of laughter or off-color remarks; becoming argumentative; and chug-a-lugging or ordering doubles.

Further drinking leads to a loss of reactions. This stage is reflected by such traits as slurring speech; fumbling with money, cigarettes, or other objects; or being unable to concentrate. The drinker's thoughts and motor skills are not synchronized.

The last stage, loss of coordination, is exhibited by stumbling and weaving, spilling drinks and dropping money, falling asleep, and a general inability to function normally.

It is important to keep drinkers out of the last two stages, because those are the stages where they can do harm to themselves and to others. Servers should be aware of the following conditions that influence the rate at which drinkers may become intoxicated, and take precautions to prevent intoxication:

- Drinking too fast
- Repeatedly ordering strong drinks
- Taking medications while drinking
- Drinking on an empty stomach
- Drinking when depressed, stressed, or exhausted

In general, females have more fatty cells than males and tend to be smaller in body size. For these reasons, they tend to absorb alcohol into their bloodstream faster than males.

When servers are aware of a drinker's need to be slowed down, they can intervene by slowing down service, not asking for reorders right away, and offering snacks. When done tactfully, the guest may not even realize what is happening.

RESPONSIBLE BUSINESS PRACTICES

For some time, the issue of liability has been a major concern to operators of alcoholic beverage establishments. A great deal has been done by state agencies, the National Restaurant Association, private training programs, and the major brewers and distillers of alcoholic beverages to educate the industry on the need for responsible business practices.

As a licensee and server of alcoholic beverages, you cannot eliminate your liability in issues involving alcohol, but you can certainly reduce your risk by establishing and adhering to responsible business practices, such as the following:

- Establish sound policies and procedures and make sure all employees are acquainted with and practice them
- Let your guests know what your policies are—put up posters and spell out your policies on table tents, menus, and wine lists
- Keep a list of all the things you do to abide by the law, such as conducting training sessions and checking IDs
- Keep an incident log at your bar, into which bartenders and servers may enter a record of incidents where they had to shut off someone or refuse service to a person
- Check the ID of anyone who does not appear to be at least 30 years old to allow a comfortable margin of safety, as opposed to trying to determine if a person is 21 years old
- Set a limit on the number of stronger drinks that may be served to a person or develop recipes for weaker versions of those drinks
- Send your servers to training programs, such as the TIPS program (Training for Intervention Procedures by Servers of Alcohol), and the ServSafe Alcohol training program
- Do not have happy hours or similar programs that encourage people to consume excessive amounts of alcohol in short periods of time

- Make nonalcoholic drinks available
- Staff adequately for peak periods, so that servers can check IDs without being rushed and monitor their guests properly
- Control the level of the lighting and music so that it does not encourage rapid drinking
- Offer free snacks to slow down consumption rates
- Offer free coffee to departing guests
- Call taxicabs or arrange for safe transportation
- Conduct periodic in-house training sessions

These kinds of activities establish you as a prudent, law-abiding businessperson who runs an ethical establishment with well-trained employees and high standards. Consequently, they can contribute positively to a legal defense, should one ever become necessary.

LIQUOR LAWS

The Alcoholic Beverage Control agency of each state and subdivision publishes its regulations, which are based on the statutes of that state. A copy of the regulations may be obtained by writing to or calling the agency. A brief summary of the regulations may be found on the government Web sites of some states. Telephone numbers and e-mail addresses (if available) of the Alcoholic Beverage Control Boards of all 50 states and the District of Columbia can be found in Appendix D. The laws and regulations vary from state to state, but two things are common across the country:

1. You cannot legally serve a minor. For the purposes of drinking, a minor is defined as any person under 21 years of age.
2. You cannot legally serve a person who is visibly intoxicated.

Checking IDs

It is imperative for a server of alcohol to check the ID of any person of questionable age. An *ID Checking Guide* may be obtained from the Drivers License Guide Co., 1492 Oddstad Drive, Redwood City, CA 94063

(800-227-8827) or online at *www.driverslicenseguide.com*. The publication describes in detail the specific features of drivers licenses of every state.

Following are some tips for checking the ID cards of persons of doubtful age:

- Hold the card in your hand; do not check it in a wallet
- Compare the picture on the ID with the face of the person
- Check the date of birth on the card and ask the person what it is
- Ask the person what their home address is
- Examine the card for signs of tampering; feel the surface and look for separations, discolorations, white-outs, or erasures
- Check the thickness of the card to determine if the picture has been substituted

DETERMINING WHO IS VISIBLY INTOXICATED

Few laws stipulate the standards for determining "visible intoxication." It is therefore important for servers to be trained to recognize the early signs of intoxication, and to act prudently to prevent guests from reaching the state of intoxication.

Action **G**uidelines

✓ Order a liquor law book from the Alcoholic Beverage Control agency of your state.

✓ Develop a policy manual for your bar.

✓ Create an outline for a training session on responsible beverage service for your employees.

14

IF YOU SUCCEED—
WHAT NEXT?

Let's say you are the one in five businesses that makes it past the fifth year. You focused on the 20 percent of the things that made 80 percent of the difference and did them well. You satisfied your target market's wants and needs, and that is why you have succeeded in business. So what happens next? Stay as you are? Expand? Franchise? Or sell, and enjoy the profits?

Many companies have started from humble beginnings and have grown to national proportions. Drive down any miracle mile and count the success stories. To decide what the right thing is for you to do, you will have to go back to square one and redefine your goals and objectives. You will have to evaluate the options and consider the sacrifices required by each. You will need to consider the implications of each possibility on your lifestyle, and decide whether it is for you.

SHOULD YOU STAY THE SAME?

Few businesses are able to remain the same for long periods of time. Even if a business is doing a good a job, external forces and changes that affect it are constantly occurring. Technology changes, consumer tastes change, new products come on to the market, economic conditions change, and new fads emerge. A business must respond to change if it is going to survive.

While some businesses have been able to adapt to changes without sacrificing the concepts that initially made them successful, managing change is one of the biggest challenges most managers face today.

SHOULD YOU EXPAND?

This question has two facets: 1) Should you expand? and 2) Can you expand? If your sales have been steadily growing and trends point to continued growth, it would seem that expansion of some sort is advisable.

But, can you expand? Do you have the physical space to enlarge your operations? If you add on to your building, can you add on to your parking lot? How would the additional space integrate with your existing production system and flow of traffic? Can new equipment be placed where it is most needed?

If a business has the funds and foresight when it initially starts up, it should consider future expansion. Extra space can be left, in critical places, to allow for expansion of a production line. Plumbing, heating, ventilation, and air-conditioning systems can be planned with an eye to the future.

It is unfortunate when a business has to move because it outgrows its present location and cannot expand there. One never knows if the dynamics that worked so well in the original setting will happen again in the new facility. Guests sometimes resent change and will try a competitor before following a business.

SHOULD YOU FRANCHISE?

This is an option that many businesses flirt with, but very few consider seriously, because it requires a great deal of legal and financial expertise, as well as a substantial amount of capital. One must be realistic in assessing whether the business, or concept, is franchisable. Does it have universal appeal? Is it unique enough to fill an existing market niche?

Many businesses open up additional company-owned locations as an alternative to franchising and all of its complexities.

SHOULD YOU SELL THE BUSINESS?

There are people who are very successful at starting and growing businesses, then selling them for substantial gains on their investment. These people enjoy the challenge of creating something from nothing, but care very little about running the business once the fun is over.

If your business does succeed, you will be in an enviable position to evaluate, without any financial pressures, whether you want to continue in it. You must ask yourself if you are happy with your lifestyle, and if you are getting the satisfaction you anticipated out of the business. If the answers to those questions are "no," you should probably sell the business, and enjoy the profit from the sale. On the other hand, if the answers are "yes," and you remain in the business and continue to do a good job, you should make a very good living and be happy in your work.

Action **G**uidelines

✓ Reassess your goals and objectives.

✓ List your various options.

✓ Tabulate, in balance sheet form, the pros and cons of each option.

✓ Select the one that most closely matches your goals and objectives.

SAMPLE BUSINESS PLAN AND LOAN APPLICATION

THE BUSINESS PLAN

Developing a business plan is a critical part of the process of starting a business. It can be used to convince investors or lenders of the soundness of a proposed business. In addition, it can be used as a business guide during the early stages of a new enterprise. Chapter 5 describes the elements of a business plan in detail. Following is an illustration of how a business plan for an upscale, urban bar and grill might appear.

BUSINESS PLAN

The Bull Market Bar & Grill
100 Finance Street
Grand City, CA 94100

November 1, 20___

John Q. Banker and James Banker (Partners)
123 Central Street
Baytown, CA 94600

Telephone:
606-555-7891

Copy No. 1

Sample Business Plan (Continued)

TABLE OF CONTENTS

Sample Business Plan (Continued)

Part Three: Supporting Documents

STATEMENT OF PURPOSE

John Q. and James Banker, copartners, seek a loan of $250,000 that, together with their combined $250,000 personal investment, will be used to acquire a license; obtain a lease at 100 Finance Street, Grand City, CA; make improvements to the leased premises; purchase furniture, fixtures, equipment, and inventories; provide working capital for two months; and cover any other preopening expenses that are necessary to open The Bull Market Bar & Grill. It is expected that the business will produce a profit in the first year, and increased profits are expected in subsequent years, ensuring a timely payback of the loan.

Part One: The Business

Background. Recognizing that the only food or beverage service near 100 Finance Street is a fast-food establishment that has a very limited menu and serves only soft drinks, the principals sensed that the needs of most of the professional occupants of the building were not being met. A survey was conducted throughout the building, which houses 1,000 employees, and it was determined that a bar and grill with healthy, light food and an upscale ambiance would be most welcome. Coupled with the fact that the new Civic Center will bring thousands of people into the area for events and conventions, it appeared a bar and grill would be very successful at this location.

The Bull Market Bar & Grill will occupy 2,400 square feet of space, and will have a capacity of 130 seats, 90 inside and 40 patio seats outside. Its hours of service will be 11 AM to 12 AM, seven days a week, however, food service will cease at 10 PM.

A piano player will play cocktail music from 6 PM to 10 PM, on Thursdays through Saturday. Other entertainment will consist of two television sets located at the bar and piped-in background music in the daytime. In the future, combos will be featured on Friday and Saturday nights, from 9 PM to 12 AM.

Mission statement. The Bull Market Bar & Grill seeks to serve high-quality food and beverages in a friendly atmosphere, while observing high standards of responsible beverage service.

Concept. The Bull Market Bar & Grill will be an upscale bar, serving liquor, beer, wine, and café food in a unique setting. Its décor will be that of a 1920s stock brokerage office, with ticker tape machines and a large blackboard showing 1929 stock prices. Dark, mahogany-paneled walls will feature poster-size pictures of famous millionaires and old front pages of the *Wall Street Journal*. Adjustable lighting will be from old-fashioned office chandeliers, and menu covers will be replicas of stock and bond certificates. Tables will have round, marble tops and sturdy captain's chairs.

Location. The business will be located at 100 Finance Street, an older office building occupied by approximately 1,000 employees of investment, law, insurance, and accounting firms. Due to the three year surplus of commercial rental space, resulting from overbuilding and the slack economy, favorable lease terms have been negotiated. A one-year lease has been arranged at $23 per square foot, with an option to renew for six years at $33 per square foot, and a subsequent eight-year renewal option to be based on consumer price index increases.

The location is one block away from the soon to be completed Civic Center. The Civic Center's conventions and events are expected to generate up to 1 million visitors annually to the city, and The Bull Market Bar & Grill will be its closest upscale bar. There will be a 1,000-car subterranean parking garage directly beneath the Civic Center. Access to The Bull Market Bar & Grill will be available from the lobby of the building and from the street.

Industry trends. Studies by several state and local agencies indicate that Grand City is emerging from its three-year period of economic sluggishness. The large infusion of tourists that will be attracted by events at the new Civic Center, coupled with the decision of two major bio-tech companies to move to Grand City, will substantially benefit the retail and hospitality sectors of the local economy. The Bull Market Bar & Grill is located in a prime position, at 100 Finance Street, to benefit from the growth.

Management. John Q. Banker will manage The Bull Market Bar & Grill. He will also function as daytime head bartender. James Banker will be head chef, and Mary L. Banker, James's sister, head waitress.

John Q. Banker has 15 years of experience as a bartender and head bartender for a major Grand City hotel and 10 years of experience as the general manager of a prominent café.

James Banker has an associate degree in hospitality management with a major in culinary arts. He has two years of experience as a bartender, and eight years of experience as a second cook and night chef for a major hotel chain.

Mary Banker has four years of waitressing experience at an upscale bar and grill in San Francisco.

Objectives and financial expectations. The immediate goal of the management team is to generate a cash flow sufficient to meet all obligations of the business and generate a before-tax net profit of 10 percent of total sales, accomplished through creative merchandising, intensive advertising, and the utilization of cost controls.

The long-term goal of the management team is to become one of Grand City's premier bars—an establishment noted for its unique ambiance, its excellent bar service, and its superb food—and to attain an annual return on investment in excess of 20 percent for its owners.

Product and service. The Bull Market Bar & Grill will be unique to the Grand City area. Its style of service and method of food presentation will be similar to that of the famous San Francisco grills, and its stock market décor will be refreshingly appealing to the targeted clientele.

The clear message at The Bull Market Bar & Grill is that "this is an excellent bar that also serves excellent food," not a restaurant that also serves drinks.

The menu will feature steaks, chops, ribs, beef kabobs, and other grill items, as well as upscale sandwich plates, such as Reubens and Monte Carlos, and taco salads, burritos, and finger foods. No other restaurant in the marketing area offers a similar grill menu.

Pricing and profitability. The Bull Market Bar & Grill's bar will operate with a bar cost percentage of 20 percent. Its grill will operate with a food cost percentage of 30 percent.

With the expected percentage breakdown of total sales to be 52 percent food sales and 48 percent beverage sales, the combined cost of sales will be 25.2 percent, producing a gross profit of 74.8 percent on total sales.

Prices will be competitive with other upscale bars. However, it is the strategy of The Bull Market Bar & Grill to give a perception of higher value than its competitors through its food and drink presentation methods.

Product life cycle. Due to the uniqueness of the stock market concept, The Bull Market Bar & Grill has an indeterminate life cycle. At the end of the business's fifth year, however, the management will conduct a self-study to determine if the concept and the menu need to be rejuvenated.

It is expected that due to normal wear and tear, the facility will need a complete refurbishing and replacement of some equipment in seven years.

Market analysis. The growth that is expected to result from the construction of the new Civic Center has been well determined by public and private research projects. One thousand employees work at 100 Finance Street. An estimated 3,000 businesspeople and retail shoppers visit the complex every business day. Seventy percent of the city's most famous specialty shops are located within three blocks of 100 Finance Street. Many people visit the complex to see the Civic Center's highly regarded architecture. Its subterranean parking garage accommodates 1,000 tourists and commuters each day because of its central location. Two universities are located in the city.

Two surveys of the occupants of the building indicate a desire for an upscale bar and grill to which they may bring business guests for food and beverages. The Bull Market Bar & Grill fills a need, and has no competition offering the same concept within its marketing area.

Competition. There are three bars, two fast-food restaurants, and a full-service restaurant within three blocks of The Bull Market Bar & Grill. One of the fast-food restaurants is located near 100 Finance Street, but has a very limited menu and no alcoholic beverage service. None of these are as easily accessible to the target clientele as The Bull Market Bar & Grill, and none offer a similar concept.

The two fast-food establishments cater mainly to youths and lower-paid retail and service workers. One of the bars is a sports bar that serves only pizza and submarine sandwiches. The other two are taverns that do not offer food menus. The full-service restaurant is a well-established, moderately priced Italian-American restaurant, with a loyal clientele. It is located on a dead-end side street and is the farthest of the five potential competitors from 100 Finance Street and the Civic Center.

Studies determined that none of the competitors presented substantial competition because of their different concepts and menu offerings.

Guests. The Bull Market Bar & Grill will have two types of guests. One is the professional and administrative workers of 100 Finance Street and nearby office buildings. The other is visitors, shoppers, tourists, and Civic Center attendees.

The first type will typically have the following characteristics: males and females, over 25, with some degree of post–high school education or training. Most of them will commute from suburban communities and will park in the underground garage. At the present time, there is no food and beverage establishment in close proximity serving the needs of this segment of the market.

The second type of guest is most likely to be discriminating diners, who prefer an upscale bar or restaurant that offers good drinks and lighter foods. They like to converse with friends and appreciate quiet background music and a unique atmosphere. They will probably be on a shopping trip or attending an event at the Civic Center. Their demographics will match closely with those of the first type of guest.

Marketing strategy. In the daytime, The Bull Market Bar & Grill will be positioned as a trendy place to bring your business and personal friends for good, light food, superb drinks, and quiet conversation—a place where you can see and be seen by important people in the business and social community; and a place where introductions and networking are common.

In the evening, it will be positioned as a unique after-work piano bar that serves excellent light food and delicious drinks. It will appeal to busy people who seek a relaxing atmosphere for socializing, as well as to tourists and patrons of Civic Center events. Contacts will be made with taxi companies, tour group leaders, and other persons who make recommendations or plan activities for tourists.

All advertisements and commercials will position The Bull Market Bar & Grill as an alternative to loud and high-energy bars. The Frankel and Franco Advertising Agency, with more then 12 years of successful experience with hospitality accounts in the Grand City area, will handle all advertising placements and public relations releases.

Support will be given to a number of charitable and community causes, and the owners of the business will be active members of the chamber of commerce, and Rotary and Kiwanis clubs.

Personnel. The staff will include 9 full-time employees and 16 part-time employees, who in total will work an average of 725 hours per week and generate an average weekly payroll of $5,262.

The estimated annual payroll of $273,626 is 26.4 percent of total sales. The following table shows the employee work schedule for The Bull Market Bar & Grill. Arrangements have been made for additional, temporary staffing on nights when special events are scheduled at the Civic Center.

EMPLOYEE WORK SCHEDULE

	Mon.	Tue.	Wed.	Thur.	Fri.	Sat.	Sun.	Total Hours	Hourly Rate	Weekly Pay
Bar Personnel										
Day Head Bartender	10/6	10/6	10/6	10/6	10/6			40	Salary	$360.00
Night Head Bartender			5/1	5/1	5/1	5/1	5/1	40	$8.00	320.00
Bartender, Part-time	10/2	10/2	10/2	10/2	10/2			20	6.00	120.00
Bartender, Part time			5/10	5/10	5/10	5/1	5/1	31	6.50	201.50
Bartender, Part-time	5/1	5/1				10/6	10/6	32	6.50	208.00
Bartender, Part-time	5/9	5/9				5/1	10/2	20	6.50	130.00
Wait Staff										
Day Head Waitperson	10/4		10/4	10/4	10/4	10/4	10/4	36	4.25	153.00
Night Head Waitperson		4/10	4/10	4/10	4/10	4/10	4/10	36	3.95	142.20
Waitperson, Part-time	10/2	10/4	10/2	10/2	10/2			22	3.15	69.30
Waitperson, Part-time	4/10	10/2	10/2	10/2	10/2			22	3.15	69.30
Waitperson, Part-time	10/2				10/2	10/2		12	3.15	37.80
Waitperson, Part-time		5/9	5/9	5/10	5/10	10/2	10/2	26	3.15	81.90
Waitperson, Part-time			5/9	5/9	5/9	5/10	5/9	21	3.15	66.15
Waitperson, Part-time	5/9					5/10	5/9	13	3.15	40.95

Kitchen Personnel

								Salary	
Head Chef	5/10		9/5	9/5	9/5	9/5	40	12.00	600.00
Night Chef	9/5	5/10	5/10	5/10	5/10	5/10	30	9.00	360.00
Rounds Person	9/5	5/10		5/10	11/7	11/7	5/11	40	9.00	360.00
Cooks Helper	5/10	5/10	5/10		5/10	5/10	5/10	30	8.50	255.00
Salad Maker	11/5	11/5	11/5	11/5		11/5	11/5	36	8.50	306.00
Dishwasher & Porter	11/5	11/5	11/5	11/5	11/5			36	8.00	288.00
Dishwasher	5/10	5/10	5/10	5/10	5/11	5/11	5/11	30	7.00	210.00

Other

								Salary	
Office Manager & Bookkeeper	9/5	9/5	9/5	9/5	9/5			40		480.00
AM Host(ess)	11/2	11/2	11/2	11/2	11/2	11/2		21	6.25	131.25
PM Host(ess)	5/8	5/8	5/8	5/8	5/8	5/8		21	6.25	131.25
Maint. & Cleaner	9/11	9/11	9/11	9/11	9/11	9/11		14	10.03	140.44

Total Weekly Payroll	$5,262.04
Times 52 Weeks	× 52
Est. Annual Payroll	$273,626.04

Risk. Risk management will be practiced from the opening day. All service employees will be required to attend an accredited Responsible Alcohol Service Course. Food service workers will all be required to take the National Food Service Sanitation Course. Both courses will entitle the bar to substantial discounts on insurance premiums.

The Bull Market Bar & Grill will carry the following insurance policies:

- Liquor liability insurance and third-party liability
- Workers' compensation insurance
- General liability insurance
- Business interruption insurance
- Product liability insurance
- Fire insurance
- Key person life insurance on partners
- Personal injury liability insurance

In addition to insuring against risk, ongoing training programs will be conducted to ensure a high degree of professionalism among employees.

LOAN APPLICATION

Loan Request and Intended Use of Funds

Applicants
John Q. Banker and James Banker (father and son, partners)
123 Central Street
Baytown, CA 94600
Telephone: 606-555-7891

Business
The Bull Market Bar & Grill
100 Finance Street
Grand City, CA 94100

Type of Business
Tavern: Serving café food and all alcoholic beverages

Size of Business
Annual sales volume of $1,035,944

Type of Ownership
General Partnership: ⅘ share John Q. Banker
⅕ share James Banker

Funds to Be Contributed by Applicants
John Q. Banker will invest $200,000 cash in the business and James Banker will invest $50,000. The equity in John Q. Banker's fully owned home, which is appraised at $450,000 (current market value), will be pledged as collateral to secure the loan.

Other Contributions by Applicants
John Q. Banker has 25 years of experience in the bar business, 15 years as a bartender and 10 years as a manager. James Banker has a college degree in food and beverage management.

Amount Requested
$250,000

Term of Loan
Fifteen years, with no prepayment penalty. First payment due three months after transaction date of loan.

Interest Rate
Bank's current lending rate—12 percent fixed rate

Debt to Equity Ratio
1 to 1 ($250,000 to $250,000)

Collateral
Mortgage on the wholly owned home of John Q. Banker. Current market value appraised at $450,000.

Other Protections
Borrowers will carry insurance against business interruption and loss due to hazards, naming the lender as a beneficiary in the event of interruption of business.

Intended Use of Funds

The partners will use the funds, in conjunction with their own investment, to acquire a license; obtain a lease; make improvements to the leased premises; purchase furniture, fixtures, equipment, and inventories necessary to open The Bull Market Bar & Grill; and conduct a Grand Opening.

Summary of Part One. John Q. Banker and his son, James Banker, seek a collateralized loan of $250,000 that, in conjunction with their combined personal investment of $250,000, will be used to open an upscale bar and grill at 100 Finance Street, Grand City. Extensive market analysis shows a need for such a facility, and a sufficient target population to sustain it. The new Civic Center, which will be located one block away, is expected to bring an additional 1 million people into the area every year.

The establishment, to be known as The Bull Market Bar & Grill, will have a capacity of 130 seats, 90 inside and 40 patio seats outside, and will offer high-quality food and beverage service in a unique atmosphere. Its décor will resemble a 1920s stock brokerage office. Surveys show it will be a welcomed alternative to the loud and rushed atmosphere of its competitors. There is no other direct competition in its dominant marketing area.

It is expected that through effective sales promotion and the use of cost controls, the business will be profitable from the first year, and will be able to pay back the loan and the partners' investment in six years.

The target market will be administrative and professional employees of 100 Finance Street and nearby office buildings, who go out to lunch every day and often entertain business guests.

Part Two: Financial Projections

START-UP REQUIREMENTS	
Cash (working capital)	$ 82,000
Leasehold Improvements	127,000
License	35,000
Beginning Inventories	
(Food, Beverages, and Supplies)	33,000
Furniture, Fixtures, and Equipment	152,660
Opening Expenses	
Liquor liability insurance, other insurances, licenses, permits, cleanup, advertising and promotion, deposits, employee training, preopening parties, and grand opening	70,340
Total Start-up Investment Required	$500,000

ESTIMATED ANNUAL SALES	
No. of Guests Expected per Week (Sum of daily estimates)	
	Total
Lunch	547
Dinner	417
Bar Drinks Only	220
Total Guests per Week	1,184
Average Menu Prices	
Sandwiches and Salads	$ 6.95
Entrées	13.45
Desserts	3.95
Drinks	4.25
Estimated Average Guest Check per Person	
Lunch: Sandwich or Salad plus Drink	$11.20
Dinner: Entrée, Salad, Dessert, plus Drinks	28.60
Bar Only: Average 2 Drinks	8.50

ESTIMATED ANNUAL SALES *(Continued)*

Estimated Weekly Sales

547 guests	×	$11.20	=	6,126
417 guests	×	28.60	=	11,926
220 guests	×	8.50	=	1,870
Total Weekly Sales				$19,922

Estimated Annual Sales

52 weeks	×	$19,922	=	$1,035,944

LIST OF FURNITURE, FIXTURES, AND EQUIPMENT

Qty.	Item	Cost
1	Ice maker, air-cooled, 600-pound capacity	$ 3,500
1	Remote, 6-keg capacity, beer refrigerator	3,500
2	Cocktail stations, 30"	2,100
2	Three-compartment bar sinks with speed	1,800
1	Direct draw, 3-keg beer box with taps	2,300
2	Post mix dispensing system, carbonator, and 50' lines	2,100
1	Three-door bar refrigerator	4,000
1	Glass froster, 3', 120-mug capacity	1,400
1	Beer bottle cooler, 4'	1,000
1	20' front bar, mahogany, granite top, and foot rail	10,500
1	14' Back bar, cabinets, mirrors, and shelves	2,800
10	Bar stools, upholstered	3,000
7	Booths, 4'	4,313
11	Lounge tables, with bases, seat 4	2,388
9	Cocktail tables, with bases, seat 2	1,750
92	Chairs	9,600
2	Television sets	4,500
	Glassware	1,100
3	Blenders	1,500
	Small bar wares and supplies	300
1	Safe, fireproof	3,000
1	Wine cellar, redwood, refrigerated	5,575
1	POS system and Cash register	10,000
1	Desk, mahogany, and swivel chair	625

LIST OF FURNITURE, FIXTURES, AND EQUIPMENT *(Continued)*

Qty.	Item	Cost
1	Desk, steel, and secretary's chair	450
1	Planter, divider, 3' high with artificial plantings	950
1	Dishwasher, automatic	11,300
1	Freezer, reach in, stainless, with racks	3,725
2	Fryers, twin basket	7,450
1	Griddle, 3'	3,500
1	Toaster, automatic, conveyor type	1,125
2	Stainless steel prep tables	800
1	Food mixer, 20 quart	4,000
1	Restaurant range	2,550
1	Convection oven	5,450
1	Garbage disposer	294
2	Refrigerators, 40 cubic feet, stainless steel	4,475
1	Fire protection hood and exhaust system	12,000
1	Broiler	2,800
	Double tank coffee maker with stand	1,800
	Chinaware and flatware	7,340
	Total Cost of Furniture, Fixtures, and Equipment	$152,660

LEASEHOLD IMPROVEMENTS

Heating, ventilation, and air-conditioning	$ 30,280
Electrical	25,920
Plumbing	25,000
Carpeting, floor and wall tile, related equipment	25,280
Carpentry, partitioning, and painting	20,520
Total Leasehold Improvements	$127,000

SOURCES AND USES OF FUNDS			
Uses of Funds	**Source of Funds**		
Start-up Expenses	**Partners' Equity**	**Loan**	**Total**
Furniture, Fixtures, and Equipment	$ 12,660	$140,000	$152,660
Leasehold Improvements	107,000	20,000	127,000
License	35,000	0	35,000
Food, Beverage, and Supplies Inventories	13,000	20,000	33,000

Opening Expenses
  Liquor liability insurance,
  other insurances, licenses,
  permits, advertising, lease
  deposit, cleanup, employee
  training, preopening parties,
  and grand opening
	60,340	10,000	70,340

Working Capital	22,000	60,000	82,000
Total Funds	$250,000	$250,000	$500,000

PROJECTED INCOME STATEMENT

The Bull Market Bar & Grill
for the period of January 1 through December 31, 20___

Sales			Percentages
Food Sales	$538,441		52.0%
Beverage Sales	497,503		48.0
Total Sales		$1,035,944	100.0
Cost of Sales			
Food Cost	$161,688		30.0
Beverage Cost	99,501		20.0
Total Cost of Sales		$261,189	25.2
Gross Profit from Operations		$774,755	74.8
Other Misc. Income		3,035	0.3
Total Income		$777,790	74.4
Controllable Expenses			
Payroll	$273,626		26.4
Employee Benefits	41,459		4.0
Direct Operating Expenses	59,078		5.7
Advertising and Promotion	30,058		2.9
Music and Entertainment	20,729		2.0
Utilities	33,166		3.2
Administrative and General Expenses	41,459		4.0
Repairs and Maintenance	20,209		2.0
Total Controllable Expenses		$519,784	50.2
Profit before Occupancy Costs		$258,006	24.3
Occupancy Costs (Triple Net)			
Rent	$57,006		5.1
Property Taxes	6,218		0.6
Other Taxes	2,073		0.2
Property Insurance	10,365		1.0
Total Occupancy Costs		$ 75,662	7.3
Profit before Interest and Depreciation		$182,344	17.0
Interest		5,115	0.5
Depreciation		20,724	2.0
Net Profit before Tax		156,505	15.1

PROJECTED INCOME STATEMENT—BY MONTH
The Bull Market Bar & Grill
for the period of January 1 through December 31, 20___

	JAN.	FEB.	MAR.	APR.	MAY	JUNE	JULY	AUG.	SEP.	OCT.	NOV.	DEC.	TOTAL
Sales													
Food	$41,600	$42,120	$43,160	$43,680	$44,200	$44,720	$45,240	$45,760	$46,280	$46,800	$47,320	$48,081	$ 538,441
Beverage	38,400	38,880	39,840	40,320	40,800	41,280	41,760	42,240	42,720	43,200	43,680	44,383	497,503
Total Sales	80,000	81,000	83,000	84,000	85,000	86,000	87,000	88,000	89,000	90,000	91,000	92,464	1,035,944
Cost of Sales													
Food	12,480	12,636	12,948	13,104	13,260	13,416	13,572	13,728	13,884	14,040	14,196	14,424	161,688
Beverage	7,680	7,776	7,968	8,064	8,160	8,256	8,352	8,448	8,544	8,640	8,736	8,877	99,501
Total Cost of Sales	20,160	20,412	20,916	21,168	21,420	21,672	21,924	22,176	22,428	22,680	22,932	23,301	261,189
Gross Profit from Operations	59,840	60,588	62,084	62,832	63,580	64,328	65,076	65,824	66,572	67,320	68,068	69,163	774,755
Other Income	240	243	249	252	255	258	261	264	267	270	273	277	3,035
Total Income	60,080	60,831	62,333	63,084	63,835	64,586	65,337	66,088	66,839	67,590	68,341	69,440	777,790
Controllable Expenses													
Payroll	21,120	21,384	21,912	22,176	22,440	22,704	22,968	23,232	23,496	23,760	24,024	24,410	273,626
Employee Benefits	3,200	3,240	3,320	3,360	3,400	3,440	3,480	3,520	3,560	3,600	3,640	3,699	41,459
Direct Operating	4,560	4,617	4,731	4,788	4,845	4,902	4,959	5,016	5,073	5,130	5,187	5,270	59,078
Advertising and Promotion	2,320	2,349	2,407	2,436	2,465	2,494	2,523	2,552	2,581	2,610	2,639	2,681	30,058

Music and Entertainment	1,600	1,620	1,660	1,680	1,700	1,720	1,740	1,760	1,780	1,800	1,820	1,849	20,729
Utilities	2,560	2,592	2,656	2,688	2,720	2,752	2,784	2,816	2,848	2,880	2,912	2,959	33,166
Administrative and General	3,200	3,240	3,320	3,360	3,400	3,440	3,480	3,520	3,560	3,600	3,640	3,699	41,459
Repairs and Maintenance	1,600	1,620	1,660	1,680	1,700	1,720	1,740	1,760	1,780	1,800	1,820	1,849	20,209
Total Controllable Expenses	40,160	40,662	41,666	42,168	42,670	43,172	43,674	44,176	44,678	45,180	45,682	46,417	519,784
Profit before Occupancy Costs	19,920	20,169	20,667	20,916	21,165	21,414	21,663	21,912	22,161	22,410	22,659	23,024	258,006
Occupancy Costs													
Rent	4,751	4,751	4,751	4,751	4,751	4,751	4,751	4,751	4,751	4,751	4,751	4,751	57,006
Property Taxes	518	518	518	518	518	518	518	518	518	518	518	518	6,218
Other Taxes	173	173	173	173	173	173	173	173	173	173	173	173	2,073
Property Insurance	864	864	864	864	864	864	864	864	864	864	864	864	10,365
Total Occupancy Expenses	6,306	6,306	6,306	6,306	6,306	6,306	6,306	6,306	6,306	6,306	6,306	6,306	75,662
Profit before Interest and Depreciation	13,614	13,863	14,361	14,610	14,859	15,108	15,357	15,606	15,855	16,104	16,353	16,718	182,344
Interest	432	432	432	432	432	432	432	432	432	432	432	365	5.115
Depreciation	1,727	1,727	1,727	1,727	1,727	1,727	1,727	1,727	1,727	1,727	1,727	1,727	20,724
NET PROFIT	11,455	11,704	12,202	12,451	12,700	12,949	13,198	13,447	13,696	13,945	14,194	14,626	156,505

CASH FLOW STATEMENT—BY MONTH
The Bull Market Bar & Grill
for the period of January 1 through December 31, 20___

SOURCES OF CASH	PRE-OPENING	JAN.	FEB.	MAR.	APR.	MAY	JUNE	JULY	AUG.	SEPT.	OCT.	NOV.	DEC.	YEAR TOTAL
Partners' Equity	$250,000													$250,000
Loan	250,000													250,000
Net Profit	0	$11,455	$11,704	$12,202	$12,451	$12,700	$12,949	$13,198	$13,447	$13,696	$13,945	$14,194	$14,564	156,505
Depreciation		1,727	1,727	1,727	1,727	1,727	1,727	1,727	1,727	1,727	1,727	1,727	1,727	20,724
TOTAL	500,000	13,182	13,431	13,929	14,178	14,427	14,676	14,925	15,174	15,423	15,672	15,921	16,291	677,229
DISBURSEMENTS														
Liquor License	35,000													35,000
Leasehold Improvements	127,000													127,000
Furn./Fix./Equip.	152,660													152,660
Beg. Inventories	33,000													33,000
Opening Costs	70,340													70,340
Monthly Loan Payments	0	0	2,500	2,500	2,500	2,500	2,500	2,500	2,500	2,500	2,500	2,500	2,500	27,500
TOTAL	418,000	0	2,500	2,500	2,500	2,500	2,500	2,500	2,500	2,500	2,500	2,500	2,500	445,500
MO. CASH FLOW	82,000	13,182	10,931	11,429	11,678	11,927	12,176	12,425	12,674	12,923	13,172	13,421	13,791	231,729
CUM. CASH FLOW	82,000	95,182	106,113	117,542	129,220	141,147	153,323	165,748	178,422	191,345	204,517	217,938	231,729	231,729

DAILY BREAK-EVEN ANALYSIS

Monthly Fixed Costs	
Occupancy Costs	$ 6,305
Salaries	6,240
Utilities	2,764
Insurance	1,864
Taxes	691
Depreciation	1,727
Total Monthly Fixed Costs	$19,591
Daily Fixed Costs (Total Monthly Fixed Cost ÷ 30 days)	$653
Daily Variable Costs	
Cost of Food (one day's supply)	$ 444
Cost of Liquor (one day's supply)	273
Cost of Wages, Benefits, and Other Controllable Expenses	1,039
Total Daily Variable Costs	$1,756
Daily Sales Volume Required to Break Even	$2,409

Conclusion and summary. This request is for a secured loan in the amount of $250,000 that, together with an investment of $250,000 by John Q. and James Banker (partners), will be used to start The Bull Market Bar & Grill. Specifically, the funds will be used to acquire a license; obtain a lease for premises at 100 Finance Street; purchase furniture, fixtures, equipment, and inventories; hire and train a staff; and for pre-opening expenses and working capital.

All financial projections have been made conservatively, with a 10 percent safety factor used to overstate most costs and to understate revenues. It is expected that The Bull Market Bar & Grill will operate profitably in its first year of operation and be able to meet all of its obligations in a timely manner.

The opening of the nearby Civic Center will attract over 1 million tourists, sports fans, and conventioneers to the dominant marketing area of The Bull Market Bar & Grill each year. This expansion of the market, coupled with aggressive marketing and strict cost controls, should enable profits to grow for the foreseeable future.

Part Three: Supporting Documents

Résumé

John Q. Banker
123 Central Street
Baytown, CA 94600
Telephone: 606-555-7891

Education
Eastern Regional High School, Baytown, CA

Employment
The Bradshaw Hotel, Grand City, CA, 1979–1994
Position: Bartender and Head Bartender

Paradise Café, Baytown, CA, 1994–2004
Position: Manager

Personal Credit References
Riverside Savings Bank
House mortgage, paid up in 2001

First State Bank, Baytown, CA
Automobile loan, 36 months, paid up in 2003

Personal
Born: April 15, 1957, Baytown, CA
Married, one son, James, and one daughter, Mary

References

Amos Lard, President
Third Institute of Savings
503 Flint Street
Grand City, CA 94100

Jeremy Vender, Sales Manager
Formidable Insurance Company
1520 Granite Road
Grand City, CA 94100

Résumé

James Banker
123 Central Street
Baytown, CA 94600
Telephone: 606-555-7891

Education

Back Bay Community College, Baytown, CA
A.S. Hospitality Management, 1994

Employment

Bradshaw Hotel, Grand City, CA, 1994–2004
Positions: Bartender, 2nd Cook, Night Chef

Personal Credit References

Prarie Savings Bank
Automobile loan, paid up in 2002

Downtown National Bank, Grand City, CA
Boat loan, 24 months, paid up in 2004

References

Angela Marsden, Executive Director
Bayside Chamber of Commerce
590 Front Street
Grand City, CA 94100

Marcia Winder, Advertising Manager
Broader & Broader Advertising Agency
117 Maynard Avenue
Grand City, CA 94100

Personal Balance Sheet
John Q. Banker
as of May 1, 20____

Assets

Cash in Bank—Savings	$ 5,000
Checking	3,000
Marketable Securities	265,000
Life Insurance (cash value)	80,000
Real Estate (current market value)	450,000
Automobile	18,000
Other Personal Assets	116,000
Total Assets	$937,000

Liabilities

Accounts Payable (kitchen renovation)	$ 19,500
Total Liabilities	$ 19,500
NET WORTH	$917,500
TOTAL LIABILITIES PLUS NET WORTH	$937,000

Personal Balance Sheet
James Banker
as of May 1, 20____

Assets

Cash in Bank—Savings	$13,300
Checking	2,500
Marketable Securities	58,000
Automobile	10,000
Other Personal Assets	6,000
Total Assets	$89,800

Liabilities

Accounts Payable	$2,100
Automobile Installment Loan	7,200
Total Liabilities	$9,300
NET WORTH	$80,500
TOTAL LIABILITIES PLUS NET WORTH	$89,800

FIGURE A.1   *Floor Plan of The Bull Market Bar & Grill*

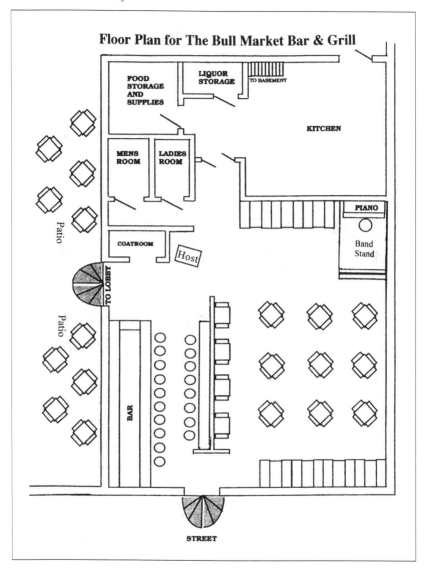

B

GLOSSARY OF BAR TERMS

Bar mats Rubber floor mats behind the bar that ease standing on a hard floor

Bar mix A liquid or powder product mixed with water to make various fruit mixes

Bar spoon A stainless steel long handle spoon used to scoop sugar or stir drinks

Bitters An aromatic, herbal compounded liquid used in certain drinks

Blend To mix certain cocktails using an electric blender

Build To make a mixed drink in an iced glass

Carafe A glass vessel with a flared mouth often used to serve house wines at a table; comes in two sizes, half liter and full liter

Cheater Also called a Fake, is made to look like a regular shot glass, but has a heavier glass bottom and sides and holds less liquor

Cherry A red, pitted Maraschino cherry

Chill To ice a glass, or refrigerate it before serving a drink in it

Club soda Also called Club, is carbonated water with a tiny bit of salt added

Collins A drink made with one part liquor, two parts Collins mix or sweet and sour mix, and topped off with soda

Coolers Made with sweet red wine and 7UP. When made with sweet white wine, soda and a lemon twist it is called a Spritzer. Both are served on ice.

Dash A shake from a bottle that produces eight to ten drops of an ingredient

Double Make it with twice as much of the principal liquor

Draught Old English for draft, and pronounced the same; refers to beer and ale dispensed from a keg through a beer tap

Dry Not to be compared with wet, it refers to lack of sweetness

Extra Dry In Martini language, it means cut down the Dry Vermouth and increase the Gin or Vodka proportionately

Flag Usually an orange slice and a Maraschino cherry on a toothpick

Flaked ice Finely crushed ice

Frappé Refers to a drink with liqueur poured over crushed ice

Frothee An additive used to create a foamy head on certain drinks

Garnish A decorative edible (in part) ornament to a drink

Ginger beer A nonalcoholic, ginger flavored, carbonated beverage

Grog An unsweetened mixture of liquors and hot or cold water

Head A foamy cap at the top of a beverage, usually beer and ale

Highball A class of drinks built in a tall glass, with a liquor and a mixer

Ice pick A four pronged hand tool used to break up ice

Jigger A one-and-one-half-ounce pour of liquor, or the device that dispenses it

Juleps A tall drink built with crushed mint leaves, sugar, flaked ice and liquor. The most popular one, the Mint Julep is made with Bourbon.

Lemon mix A powder mixed with water to produce a sweet/sour liquid mix; may be purchased in ready-to-use liquid form

Lemon twist A strip of lemon peel that is twisted to emit flavoring agents

Lime juice A commercially bottled lime juice product, such as Rose's. Rarely are fresh limes squeezed (other than lime wedges) in house.

Margarita salt Kosher salt or other coarsely ground salt; used for rimming glass

Mist Drink made with liquor poured over flaked or finely crushed ice

Muddler A wooden pestle used to crush fruit garnishes in a glass

Neat An undiluted liquor poured straight into an unchilled glass

On the rocks A liquor or liqueur served over ice cubes

POS system A computerized point-of-sale terminal that replaces a cash register and may be integrated with peripheral devices that can seamlessly handle every aspect of a transaction

Post mix Concentrated soft drink syrups to which carbonated water is added mechanically when the product is dispensed

Pour mat A rubber mat, set on the rail of a bar, on which drinks are made

Pour spout A spout inserted in bottles, to pour liquor at an ever rate

Pousse café A layered drink, of three or more liqueurs, served in small glass

Pre-mix Soft drink beverages that are ready to dispense, not concentrated

Presbyterian A highball made with a liquor, and half ginger ale and half soda

Punch Made with sweetened milk, sugar, and a liquor; served hot or cold (Term is now used more often in reference to fruit punches)

Quinine water Same as tonic water

Rimming Applying sugar or salt to the rim of a premoistened glass

Rocks Nickname for ice cubes

Seltzer Carbonated water, like club soda, but no salt added

Shaker A steel mixing cap, used on a glass mixing cup for shaking drinks

Shooter A shot of requested liqueur or liquor, usually drunk in one gulp

Shot Typically, a one-ounce pour of liquor directly into a shot glass

Simple syrup A sweetener made with equal parts of sugar and boiling water

Sling A tall drink made with liquor or liqueur, sweetened lemon mix and a splash of soda; sometimes topped with cherry brandy

Soda water Also called club soda; like seltzer, but contains a bit of salt

Sour mix Sweetened lemon juice, with albumin added to create some foam

Speed cup A short metal shaker

Speed pourer Like a pour spout, but dispenses beverage faster

Splash A quick pour done with a flick of the wrist

Spritzer White wine and soda served on ice cubes in a large wine glass

Strainer A metal tool used to strain ice from a drink while pouring into glass

Straight up Strain the drink into a cocktail glass right after having mixed it

Swizzle stick A stirring tool for guest pleasure; also used as an advertising medium

Tall An ordering term for a drink to be served in a tall glass

Tonic water A carbonated mixer, flavored with quinine; bitter sweet, citrus

Up Same as straight-up

Virgin A term for requesting any drink, without any alcoholic ingredient, such as a Virgin Mary (no vodka in it)

Well liquor Also called bar brands or house liquor; refers to less expensive liquors of the seven basic types that are kept in wells or speed racks and automatically served when a guest does not specify a preferred liquor

DRINK RECIPES

The following drink recipes have passed the test of time and are served in many fine bars from coast to coast. Some may have regional variations. With the addition of locally popular drinks, this list constitutes the basis of a fine repertoire for a bartender. Current consumption patterns indicate that cocktails are becoming increasingly popular among younger adults.

ALABAMA SLAMMER

Fill Collins glass with ice cubes
½ oz. Southern Comfort
½ oz. Amaretto
½ oz. Sloe Gin
Fill with lemon mix and shake
Serve with an orange slice and a
   cherry on a pick

AMARETTO AND COFFEE

Goblet or mug
1 oz. Amaretto
Fill with hot black coffee
Top with whipped cream and serve

ANGEL TIP

Cordial glass
¾ full with brown Crème de Cacao
Float heavy cream on top
Serve with a cherry on a pick

BACARDI COCKTAIL

Cocktail glass, chilled
1 oz. Bacardi light rum
½ oz. Grenadine
1½ oz. lemon/lime mix
Shake or blend, and strain into
glass
Garnish with a lime wedge

B & B

Snifter glass
½ oz. Benedictine
½ oz. Brandy (Cognac recommended)
*(Brandy and Benedictine also can be
purchased premixed, and may be
poured directly from the bottle.)*

B-52

Cordial glass
⅓ Kahlua
⅓ Irish Cream Liqueur
⅓ Grand Marnier
Layer in order shown

BLACK RUSSIAN

Fill Rocks glass with ice cubes
1½ oz. Vodka
½ oz. Kahlua
Stir and serve

BLOODY MARY

Fill Highball or Collins glass
with ice cubes
Dash of Worcestershire and
Tabasco
1 oz. Vodka
Fill with tomato juice
Garnish with a celery spear or a
lime wedge

BOURBON MANHATTAN

Cocktail or Rocks glass
½ oz. sweet Vermouth
1½ oz. Bourbon
Stir and serve with a cherry

BRANDY ALEXANDER

Champagne Saucer glass, chilled
1 oz. Brandy
1 oz. brown Crème de Cacao
1 oz. cream
Shake or blend, and strain into
glass
Sprinkle with nutmeg

BURNT ALMOND

Fill Highball glass with ice cubes
½ oz. Kahlua
½ oz. Amaretto
½ oz. Vodka
Fill with milk
Shake or speed cup

CALIFORNIA ROOT BEER

Fill Highball glass with ice cubes
½ oz. Kahlua
½ oz. Galliano
Fill with soda
Serve

CAPE CODDER

Fill Highball glass with ice cubes
1 oz. Vodka
Fill with cranberry juice
Serve with a lime wedge

CHAMPAGNE COCKTAIL

Champagne Saucer glass
1 cube sugar
2 dashes bitters, on sugar cube
Fill with Champagne
Serve with a lemon twist

CHOCOLATE-MINT MARTINI

Cocktail glass
1 oz. Vodka
½ oz. white Crème de Menthe
½ oz. white Crème de Cacao
Shake with ice, and strain into
    glass
Serve with a mint sprig or a
    chocolate stick

CLAM DIGGER

Fill Highball glass with ice cubes
1 oz. Vodka
Fill with Clamato juice
Serve with a lime wedge

COSMOPOLITAN #1

Cocktail or Rocks glass
1 oz. Vodka
½ oz. Triple Sec (or Cointreau)
½ oz. Rose's lime juice
½ oz. cranberry juice
Shake or blend
Garnish with a lime wedge

CREAMSICLE

Fill Highball glass with ice cubes
½ oz. Triple Sec
½ oz. white Crème de Cacao
1 oz. Vodka
Almost fill with milk
Shake or blend, and strain into
    glass
Top off with orange juice

DAIQUIRI

Cocktail glass, chilled
1 oz. light Rum
2 oz. lemon/lime mix
Shake or blend, and strain into
    glass
Garnish with a lime wedge
*(For frozen Daiquiris: Substitute one
scoop of crushed ice and blend to
consistency of slush)*

DRY BOURBON MANHATTAN

Cocktail or Rocks glass
½ oz. dry Vermouth
1½ oz. Bourbon
Stir and serve with a twist

DRY MANHATTAN

Cocktail or Rocks glass
½ oz. dry Vermouth
1½ oz. Whiskey
Stir and serve with a twist

DRY ROB ROY

Cocktail or Rocks glass
½ oz. dry Vermouth
1½ oz. Scotch
Stir and serve with a lemon twist

EXTRA DRY MARTINI

Same as Martini but reduce the
Vermouth by ¼ oz. and increase
the liquor by ¼ oz.

FUZZY NAVEL

Fill Highball glass with ice cubes
1 oz. Peach Schnapps
Fill with orange juice
Stir and serve

GALLIANO STINGER

Cocktail or Rocks glass
1½ oz. Brandy
½ oz. Galliano
Shake and serve straight up or on
the rocks

GIBSON

Same as martini, except garnish
with a cocktail onion

GIN AND TONIC

Fill Highball glass with ice
1 oz. Gin
Fill with tonic water (Quinine
water)
Serve with a lime wedge

GIN GIMLET

Cocktail or Rocks glass
1½ oz. Gin
½ oz. Rose's lime juice
Stir and serve with a lime wedge

GIRL SCOUT COOKIE

Fill Highball glass with ice cubes
½ oz. Kahlua
½ oz. white Crème de Cacao
½ oz. green Crème de Menthe
Fill with milk
Shake and serve

GODFATHER

Fill Rocks glass with ice cubes
1½ oz. Scotch
½ oz. Amaretto
Stir and serve

GODMOTHER

Fill Rocks glass with ice cubes
1½ oz. Vodka
½ oz. Amaretto
Stir and serve

GODSON

Fill Rocks glass with ice cubes
1½ oz. Brandy
½ oz. Amaretto

GOLDEN CADILLAC

Champagne Saucer glass
1 oz. Galliano
1 oz. white Crème de Cacao
1 oz. cream
Shake or blend, and strain into
glass

GOLDEN DREAM

Champagne Saucer glass, chilled
½ oz. Galliano
½ oz. Triple Sec (or Cointreau)
1 oz. orange juice
1 oz. cream
Shake or blend, and strain into
glass

GRAPE CRUSH

Fill Highball glass with ice cubes
1 oz. Vodka
½ oz. Chambord (or raspberry
liqueur)
Almost fill with lemon mix and
shake
Top off with splash of 7UP

GRASSHOPPER

Champagne Saucer glass, chilled
1 oz. green Crème de Menthe
1 oz. white Crème de Cacao
1 oz. cream
Shake or blend, and strain into
glass

HAIRY NAVEL

Fill Highball glass with ice cubes
1 oz. Peach Schnapps
½ oz. Vodka
Fill with orange juice
Stir and serve

HARVEY WALLBANGER

Fill Highball glass with ice cubes
1 oz. Vodka
Almost fill with orange juice
Top with Galliano and serve

INTERNATIONAL STINGER

Cocktail or Rocks glass
1½ oz. Metaxa Brandy
½ oz. Galliano
Serve straight up or on the rocks

IRISH COFFEE

Goblet or mug
Sugar (1 barspoon)
1 oz. Irish Whiskey
Fill with hot black coffee
Top with whipped cream and
serve

KAMIKAZI

Fill Rocks glass with ice cubes
1 oz. Vodka
½ oz. Triple Sec
½ oz. Rose's lime juice
Serve with a lime wedge

LONG ISLAND ICED TEA

Fill Collins glass with ice cubes
½ oz. each of Vodka, Gin, Rum,
Tequila, and Triple Sec
Fill with lemon mix and shake
Splash with cola
Garnish with a lemon wedge
(Bars often limit guests to two.)

MADRAS

Fill Highball glass with ice cubes
1 oz. Vodka
Half fill with orange juice
Half fill with cranberry juice
Serve with a lime wedge

MANHATTAN

Cocktail or Rocks glass
½ oz. sweet Vermouth
1½ oz. Whiskey
Stir and serve with a cherry

MARGARITA

Cocktail or Coupe glass, rimmed
  with salt
1½ oz. Tequila
½ oz. Triple Sec
1 oz. lemon/lime mix
Shake or blend, and strain into
  glass
Garnish with a lime wedge and
  serve
*(For frozen Margaritas: Add one scoop
of crushed ice and blend to consistency
of slush)*

MARTINI (TRADITIONAL)

Cocktail or Rocks glass
½ oz. dry Vermouth
1½ oz. Gin
Stir and serve with an olive or a
  twist

MELON BALL

Fill Collins glass with ice cubes
1 oz. Vodka
1 oz. Melon Liqueur
Fill with orange juice
Serve with an orange slice and a
  cherry on a pick

MIMOSA

Wine glass, chilled
Half fill with Champagne
Half fill with orange juice
Do not stir

MUDSLIDE (ORIGINAL)

Fill Rocks glass with ice cubes
1 oz. Vodka
1 oz. Kahlua
1 oz. Irish Cream Liqueur
Pour ingredients in order
(Resembles a mudslide as it drizzles down)

OLD FASHIONED

Rocks glass
1 cube of sugar and
2 dashes of bitters
Add an orange slice and a cherry, and muddle all together
1½ oz. Whiskey, Scotch, or Bourbon
Fill with ice cubes and soda

PEARL HARBOR

Fill Collins glass with ice cubes
1 oz. Melon liqueur
1 oz. Vodka
Fill with pineapple juice and shake
Serve with a pineapple chunk

PERFECT BOURBON MANHATTAN

Cocktail or Rocks glass
¼ oz. dry Vermouth
¼ oz. sweet Vermouth
1½ oz. Bourbon
Stir and serve with a twist

PERFECT MANHATTAN

Cocktail or Rocks glass
¼ oz. dry Vermouth
¼ oz. sweet Vermouth
1½ oz. Whiskey
Stir and serve with a twist

PERFECT ROB ROY

Cocktail or Rocks glass
¼ oz. dry Vermouth
¼ oz. sweet Vermouth
1½ oz. Scotch
Stir and serve with a twist

PINA COLADA

Fill Highball glass with ice cubes
1½ oz. light Rum
Fill with Piña Colada mix and shake
Serve with a pineapple chunk

PINK LADY #1

Champagne saucer glass, chilled
1 oz. Gin
½ oz. Grenadine
1½ oz. cream
Shake or blend, and strain into glass

PINK SQUIRREL

Champagne saucer glass, chilled
1 oz. Crème de Almond (Noyaux)
1 oz. white Crème de Cacao
1 oz. cream
Shake or blend, and strain into
glass

PLANTERS PUNCH

Fill Collins glass with ice cubes
1 oz. dark Rum
½ oz. Grenadine
1½ oz. orange juice
1½ oz. lemon mix
Shake with speed cup
Garnish with an orange slice and a
cherry on a pick

PRESBYTERIAN (PRESS)

Fill Highball glass with ice cubes
1 oz. liquor (Bourbon, Scotch, or
Whiskey)
Half fill with soda
Half fill with Ginger Ale
Serve

ROB ROY

Cocktail or Rocks glass
½ oz. sweet Vermouth
1½ oz. Scotch
Stir and serve with a cherry

RUM AND COKE

Fill Highball glass with ice cubes
1 oz. Rum
Fill with cola and serve
*(Add a lime wedge and it becomes a
Cuba Libre)*

RUSTY NAIL

Fill Rocks glass with ice cubes
1½ oz. Scotch
½ oz. Drambuie
Stir and serve

SALTY DOG

Rim Highball glass with salt and
fill with ice cubes
1 oz. Vodka
Fill with grapefruit juice and serve
(Without salt it's a Grey Hound)

SCARLET O'HARA

Cocktail glass
1 oz. Southern Comfort
1 oz. cranberry juice
1 oz. lemon mix
Shake with ice, and strain and
serve

SCREWDRIVER

Fill Highball glass with ice cubes
1 oz. Vodka
Fill with orange juice and serve

SEABREEZE

Fill Highball glass with ice cubes
1 oz. Vodka
Half fill with grapefruit juice
Half fill with cranberry juice
Serve with a lime wedge

SEVEN AND SEVEN

Fill Highball glass with ice
1 oz. Seagram's Seven whiskey
Fill with 7UP or lemon flavored
    soda
Serve

SEX ON THE BEACH

Fill Highball glass with ice cubes
1 oz. Vodka
½ oz. Peach Schnapps
Fill with equal parts cranberry
    juice and orange juice
Stir and serve

SIDECAR

Cocktail glass, chilled, rimmed
    with sugar
1½ oz. Brandy
½ oz. Triple Sec (or Cointreau)
1 oz. lemon mix
Shake or blend, and strain into
    glass
Serve

TEQUILA SUNRISE

Fill Highball glass with ice cubes
1 oz. Tequila
Almost fill with orange juice
Top with ½ oz. Grenadine
Serve

TEQUILA SUNSET

Same as Sunrise except use grape-
    fruit juice instead of orange juice

TOASTED ALMOND

Fill Highball glass with ice cubes
½ oz. Kahlua
½ oz. Amaretto
Fill with milk
Shake with speed cup and serve

TOM COLLINS

Fill Collins glass with ice cubes
1 oz. Gin
2 oz. lemon mix
Shake with speed cup
Top with soda
Garnish with an orange slice and a
    cherry on a pick

VODKA GIMLET

Cocktail or Rocks glass
1½ oz. Vodka
½ oz. Rose's lime juice
Stir and serve with a lime wedge

VODKA MARTINI

Cocktail or Rocks glass
½ oz. dry Vermouth
1½ oz. Vodka
Stir and serve with an olive or a
   twist

WARD EIGHT

Sour glass, chilled
1 oz. Whiskey
½ oz. Grenadine
1½ oz. lemon mix
Shake or blend, and strain into
   glass
Garnish with an orange slice and a
   cherry on a pick

WHISKEY SOUR

Chilled sour glass
1 oz. Whiskey
2 oz. lemon mix
Shake or blend, and strain into
   glass
Garnish with an orange slice and a
   cherry on a pick

WHITE RUSSIAN
(ORIGINAL VERSION)

Fill Rocks glass with ice cubes
1½ oz. Vodka
½ oz. Kahlua
Float heavy cream on top
*(Many bars are now shaking this
drink and serving it in a Highball
glass.)*

WINE COOLER

Fill large wine glass with ice cubes
Fill two-thirds with sweet red wine
Fill one-third with 7UP or lemon
   flavored soda
Serve

WOO WOO

Highball glass filled with ice cubes
1 oz. Peach Schnapps
½ oz. Vodka
Fill with cranberry juice and serve

STATE ALCOHOLIC BEVERAGE CONTROL BOARDS

Following is a list of the state agencies that administer and enforce the laws and regulations regarding licensing and the production, distribution, and service of alcoholic beverages.

Alabama
Alcoholic Beverage Control
  Board in Montgomery
Telephone: 334-271-3840
E-mail: *rvp@abcboard.state.al.us*

Alaska
Alcoholic Beverage Control
  Board in Anchorage
Telephone: 907-269-0350
E-mail: *William_roche@revenue.
  state.ak.us*

Arizona
Department of Liquor License
  and Control in Phoenix
Telephone: 602-542-9030
E-mail: *hamiltos@ll.state.az.us*

Arkansas
Alcoholic Beverage Control
  Division in Little Rock
Telephone: 501-682-1105
E-mail: *Milton.lueken@dfa.state.ar.us*

California
Department of Alcoholic
  Beverage Control in Sacramento
Telephone: 916-419-2500
E-mail: *cust.serv@abc.ca.gov*

Colorado
Liquor Enforcement Division
  in Denver
Telephone: 303-205-2300
E-mail: *nhamby@spike.dor.state.co.us*

Connecticut
Department of Consumer
  Protection
Telephone: 860-713-6200
E-mail: *liquor.control@po.state.ct.us*

Delaware
Office of the Alcoholic Beverage
  Control Commissioner
Telephone: 302-577-5222
Web URL: *http://dabcte.state.de.us/
  dabcpublic/index.jsp*

District of Columbia
Alcoholic Beverage Control
  Board in D.C.
Telephone: 202-442-4423
E-mail: *abra@dc.gov*

Florida
Div. of Alcoholic Beverages &
  Tobacco in Tallahassee
Telephone: 850-488-3227
E-mail: *molina@mail.dbpr.state.fl.us*

Georgia
Alcohol & Tobacco Law
  Enforcement Division
Telephone: 404-417-4867
E-mail: *ronjohnson@dor.ga.gov*

Hawaii
Department of Taxation
Telephone: 808-587-4242
E-mail: *taxpayer.services@hawaii.gov*

Idaho
Alcoholic Beverage Control
  in Meridian
Telephone: 208-884-7060
E-mail: *abc@isp.idaho.gov*

Illinois
Illinois Liquor Control
  Commission
Telephone: 312-814-0773
E-mail: *Lee_Roupas@cms.state.il.us*

Indiana
Indiana Alcohol and Tobacco
  Commission
Telephone: 317-232-2430
E-mail: *comments@atc.in.gov*

Iowa
Iowa Alcoholic Beverage Division
  in Ankeny
Telephone: 515-281-7414
E-mail: *seib@iowaabd.com*

Kansas
Alcohol Beverage Control
  Division in Topeka
Telephone: 785-296-7015
E-mail: *abc_mail@kdor.state.ks.us*

Kentucky
Office of Alcoholic Beverage
  Control in Frankfort
Telephone: 502-564-4850
E-mail: *enforcement-jim.acquisto@
  mail.state.ky.us*

Louisiana
Office of Alcohol and Tobacco
  Control
Telephone: 225-925-4041
E-mail: *keith.bernard@la.gov*

Maine
Bureau of Liquor Enforcement
  and Licensing in Augusta
Telephone: 207-624-8973
E-mail: *laurence.d.sanborn@state.*
  me.us

Maryland
Alcohol & Tobacco Tax Bureau
  in Annapolis
Telephone: 410-260-7314
E-mail: *att@comp.state.md.us*

Massachusetts
Alcoholic Beverages Control
  Commission in Boston
Telephone: 617-727-3040
E-mail: *rbailey@tre.state.ma.us*

Michigan
Liquor Control Commission
  in Lansing
Telephone: 517-322-1400
E-mail: *mlccinfo2@michigan.gov*

Minnesota
Minnesota Dept. of Public Safety
  Alcohol and Gambling
Telephone: 651-296-6159
E-mail: *Al.Erickson@state.mn.us*

Mississippi
Alcohol Beverage Control
Telephone: 601-856-1301
E-mail: *mhicks@mstc.state.ms.us*

Missouri
Division of Alcohol and Tobacco
  Control in Jefferson City
Telephone: 573-751-2333
E-mail: *steve.shimmen@dps.mo.gov*

Montana
Customer Service Center,
  Liquor Licensing
Telephone: 406-444-6900
E-mail: *jaswood@state.mt.us*

Nebraska
Liquor Control Commission
  in Lincoln
Telephone: 402-471-2571
Web URL: *www.nol.org/home/nlcc*

Nevada
Department of Taxation
Telephone: 775-684-2000
Web URL: *http://tax.state.nv.us/*

New Hampshire
State Liquor Commission in
  Concord
Telephone: 603-271-3521
E-mail: *info@liquor.state.nh.us*

New Jersey

The Div. of Alcoholic Beverage
Control
Telephone: 609-984-2830
E-mail: *abcwebinfo@lps.state.nj.us*

New Mexico

Alcohol and Gaming Division
in Santa Fe
Telephone: 505-827-7066
Web URL: *www.rld.state.nm.us.agd/*

New York

State Liquor Authority in Albany
Telephone: 518-486-4767
Web URL: *www.state.ny.us*

North Carolina

Alcoholic Beverage Control
Commission in Raleigh
Telephone: 919-779-0700
E-mail: *contactus@ncabc.com*

North Dakota

Office of Attorney General
in Bismarck
Telephone: 701-328-2329
E-mail: *ndag@state.nd.us*

Ohio

Dept. of Commerce, Div. of
Liquor Control in Columbus
Telephone: 614-644-2360
E-mail: *public@liquor.state.oh.us*

Oklahoma

Alcoholic Beverage Laws
Enforcement Commission in
Oklahoma City
Telephone: 405-521-3484
E-mail: *ablecomm@mhs.state.ok.us*

Oregon

Oregon Liquor Control
Commission
Telephone: 503-872-5000
E-mail: *joy.center@state.or.us*

Pennsylvania

Pennsylvania Liquor Control
Board in Harrisburg
Telephone: 717-787-5230
Web URL: *www.lcb.state.pa.us*

Rhode Island

Dept. of Business Regulation
in Providence
Telephone: 401-222-2562
E-mail: *commerciallicensinginquiry@dbr.state.ri.us*

South Carolina

Dept. of Revenue, Regulatory
Div., in Columbia
Telephone: 803-898-5172

South Dakota

Dept. of Revenue and
Regulations, Special Tax Div.
in Pierre
Telephone: 605-773-3311
E-mail: *specialt@state.sd.us*

Tennessee

Alcoholic Beverage Commission
in Nashville
Telephone: 615-741-1602
Web URL: *www.state.tn.us*

Texas

Alcoholic Beverage Commission
Headquarters in Austin
Telephone: 1-888-THE-TABC
Web URL: *www.tabc.state.tx.us*

Utah

Utah Dept. of Alcoholic Beverage
Control
Telephone: 801-977-6800
E-mail: *hotline@utah.gov*

Vermont

Dept. of Liquor Control in
Montpelier
Telephone: 802-828-2339
E-mail: *enforcement@dlc.state.vt.us*

Virginia

Alcoholic Beverage Control
Board in Richmond
Telephone: 804-213-4400
E-mail: *spwalkr@abc.state.va.us*

Washington

Washington State Liquor
Control Board
Telephone: 360-664-1727
E-mail: *ks@liq.wa.gov*

West Virginia

West Virginia Alcohol Beverage
Control Commission
Telephone: 304-558-2481
E-mail: *grobinson@abcc.state.wv.us*

Wisconsin

Alcohol-Tobacco Enforcement
Unit in Madison
Telephone: 608-266-6757
E-mail: *rjohnso2@dor.state.wi.us*

Wyoming

Liquor Division in Cheyenne
Telephone: 307-777-6453
E-mail: *tmonto@state.wy.us*

E

STATE RESTAURANT ASSOCIATIONS

Alabama Restaurant Association
61B Market Place
Montgomery, AL 36124-1413
334-244-1320

Alaska Cabaret, Hotel, Restaurant & Retailers Association
1111 East 80th Avenue, Ste.3
Anchorage, AK 99518
907-274-8133

Arizona Restaurant & Hospitality Association Foundation
2400 N. Central Avenue, Suite 109
Phoenix, AZ 85004
602-307-9134

Arkansas Hospitality Association
P.O. Box 3866
Little Rock, AR 72203
501-376-2323

California Restaurant Association Educational Foundation
1011 10th Street
Sacramento, CA 95814
916-431-2747

Colorado Restaurant Association Education Fund
430 East 7th Avenue
Denver, CO 80203
303-830-2972

Connecticut Restaurant Association
100 Roscommon Park, Suite 320
Middletown, CT 06457
860-635-5600

Delaware Restaurant Association
P.O. Box 8004
Newark, DE 19714
302-227-7300

Florida Restaurant Association
230 South Adams Street
Tallahassee, FL 32301
850-224-2250

Georgia Restaurant Association
480 East Paces Ferry Rd, Ste 7
Atlanta, GA 30305
404-467-9000

Hawaii Restaurant Association
1451 S King Street, Suite 503
Honolulu, HI 96814
808-536-9105

Hospitality Association of South Carolina
1338 Main Street, Ste. 505
Columbia, SC 29201
803-765-9000

Idaho Lodging & Restaurant Association
134 South 5th Street
Boise, ID 83702
208-342-0777

Illinois Restaurant Association
200 North LaSalle St., Ste. 880
Chicago, IL 60601
312-787-4000

Iowa Hospitality Association Educational Foundation
8525 Douglas Avenue, Suite 47
Des Moines, IA 50322
515-276-1454

Kansas Restaurant and Hospitality Association Ed. Found.
359 South Hydraulic
Wichita, KS 67211
316-267-8383

Kentucky Restaurant Association
133 Evergreen Road, #201
Louisville, KY 40243
502-896-0464

Louisiana Restaurant Association Education Foundation
2700 North Arnoult Road
Metairie, LA 70002
504-454-2277

Maine Restaurant Association
Five Wade Street
P.O. Box 5060
Augusta, ME 04332-5060
207-623-2178

Maryland Restaurant
Association
6301 Hillside Court
Columbia, MD 21046
410-290-6800

Massachusetts Restaurant
Association Hospitality
Institute
Southborough Technology Park,
    333 Turnpike Road, Suite 102
Southborough, MA 01772-1775
508-303-9905

Michigan Restaurant
Association
225 West Washtenaw St.
Lansing, MI 48933
517-482-5244

Minnesota Restaurant
Association
305 East Roselawn Avenue
St. Paul, MN 55117
651-778-2400

Mississippi Restaurant
Association
130 Riverview Drive, Suite A
Flowood, MS 39232
601-420-4210

Missouri Restaurant
Association
1810 Craig Road, Ste. 225
St. Louis, MO 63146
314-576-2777

Montana Restaurant
Association
1537 Avenue D, Ste. 320
Billings, MT 59102
406-256-1005

Nebraska Restaurant
Association
P.O. Box 83086
Lincoln, NE 68501-3086
402-488-3999

Nevada Restaurant Association
1500 E. Tropicana Avenue,
    Suite 114-A
Las Vegas, NV 89119

New Hampshire Lodging &
Restaurant Assn.
14 Dixon Avenue, Ste. 208
Concord, NH 03301
603-228-9585

New Jersey Restaurant
Association
126 West State Street
Trenton, NJ 08608
609-599-3316

New Mexico Restaurant
Association
9201 Montgomery Blvd, NE,
    Suite 602
Albuquerque, NM 87111
505-343-9848

New York State Restaurant
Association
409 New Karner Road
Albany, NY 12205
518-452-4222

North Carolina Restaurant
Association
204 West Millbrook Road
Raleigh, NC 27609-4304
919-844-0098

North Dakota Hospitality
Association
P.O. Box 428
Bismark, ND 58502
701-223-2284

Ohio Restaurant Association
1525 Bethel Road, Ste. 301
Columbus, OH 43220
614-442-3535

Oklahoma Restaurant
Association
3800 North Portland
Oklahoma City, OK 73112-2948
405-942-8181

Oregon Restaurant
AssociationEducational
Foundation
8565 SW Salish Lane, Ste. 120
Wilsonville, OR 97070
503-682-4422

Pennsylvania Restaurant
Association
100 State Street
Harrisburg, PA 17101-1024
717-232-4433

Restaurant & Hospitality
Association of Indiana
200 South Meridian,
   Suite 350
Indianapolis, IN 46225-1076
317-673-4211

Restaurant Association of
Metro Washington, Inc.
1200 17th Street, N.W.
   Suite 110
Washington, DC 20036
202-331-5990

Rhode Island Hospitality &
Tourism Association
832 Dyer Avenue
Cranston, RI 02920
401-223-1120

South Dakota Retailers
Association—Restaurant
Division
3612 Landmark Drive, Suite B
Columbia, SD 29204
605-224-5050

Tennessee Restaurant
Association
720 Cool Springs Boulevard,
　Suite 150
Franklin, TN 37067
615-771-7056

Texas Restaurant Association
1400 Lavaca
Austin, TX 78701
512-457-4100

Utah Restaurant Association
420 East South Temple, #355
Salt Lake City, UT 84111
801-322-0123

Vermont Lodging & Restaurant
Association
13 Kilburn Street
Burlington, VT 05401
802-660-9001

Virginia Hospitality & Travel
Association
2101 Libbie Avenue
Richmond, VA 23230-2621
804-288-3065

Washington Restaurant
Association Education
Foundation
510 Plum Street Southeast,
　Suite 200
Olympia, WA 98501-1587
360-956-7279

West Virginia Hospitality &
Travel Association
P.O. Box 2391
Charleston, WV 25311
304-342-6511

Wisconsin Restaurant
Association Education
Foundation
2801 Fish Hatchery Rd.
Madison, WI 53713
608-270-9950

Wyoming Restaurant
Association
211 West 19th, Ste. 201
Cheyenne, WY 82001
307-634-8816

STATE
HEALTH DEPARTMENTS

Following is a list of state agencies that issue permits and regulate and enforce the public health laws of the state.

Alabama
Dept. of Public Health
201 Monroe Street
Montgomery, AL 36104
334-206-5200

Alaska
Div. of Public Health
Dept. of Health & Social Services
P.O. Box 110601
Juneau, AK 99811
907-465-3030

Arizona
Dept. of Health Services
150 North 18th Avenue
Phoenix, AZ 85007
602-542-1001

Arkansas
Dept. of Health
4815 West Markham Street
Little Rock, AR 72205
501-682-2111

California
Health & Human Services Agency
1600 9th Street, Room 460
Sacramento, CA 95814
916-654-3345

Colorado
Dept. of Public Health & Environ.
4300 Cherry Creek Drive, South
Denver, CO 80246
303-692-2100

Connecticut
Dept. of Public Health
410 Capitol Avenue
Hartford, CT 06106
860-509-7101

Delaware
Dept. of Health & Social Services
Herman Holloway Sr. Campus
1901 North Depont Highwy,
    Main Bldg.
Newcastle, DE 19720
302-255-9040

Florida
Dept. of Health
2585 Merchants Row Boulevard,
    Suite 140
Tallahassee, FL 32399
850-245-4321

Georgia
Div. of Public Health.
2 Peachtree Street, NW
Atlanta, GA 30303
404-657-2700

Hawaii
Dept. of Health
P.O. Box 3378
Honolulu, HI 96801
808-586-4410

Idaho
Dept. of Health & Welfare
450 West State Street
Peter T. Cenarrusa Building
Boise, ID 83720
208-334-5500

Illinois
Dept. of Public Health
535 West Jefferson Street, 5th Floor
Springfield, IL 62761
217-782-4977

Indiana
State Dept. of Health
2 North Meridian Street
Indianapolis, IN 46204
317-233-7400

Iowa
Dept. of Public Health
Lucas Building, 321 East
    12th Street
Des Moines, IA 50319
515-281-8474

Kansas
Dept. of Health & Environment
1000 S.W. Jackson, Suite 540
Topeka, KS 66612
785-296-0461

Kentucky
Cabinet for Health and Family
    Services
275 East Main Street
Frankfort, KY 40601
502-564-7042

Louisiana
Dept. of Health & Hospitals
1201 Capitol Access Road
P.O. Box 629
Baton Rouge, LA 70821
225-342-9500

Maine
Dept. of Human Services
State House Station #11
Augusta, ME 04333
207-287-2736

Maryland
Dept. of Health & Mental Hygiene
201 West Preston Street, 5th Floor
Baltimore, MD 21201
410-767-6505

Massachusetts
Dept. of Public Health
250 Washington Street
Boston, MA 02108
617-624-5200

Michigan
Dept. of Community Health
Lewis Cass Building, 6th Floor
320 South Walnut
Lansing, MI 48913
517-373-0408

Minnesota
Dept. of Health
85 East 7th Place, Suite 400
St. Paul, MN 55101
651-215-5806

Mississippi
State Department of Health
P.O. Box 1700
Jackson, MS 39215
601-576-7400

Missouri
Dept. of Health
920 Wildwood, P.O. Box 570
Jefferson City, MO 65102
573-751-6001

Montana
Dept. of Health & Human Services
111 North Sanders, Room 301/308
Helena, MT 59601
406-444-5622

Nebraska
Dept. of Health
P.O. Box 95007
Lincoln, NE 68509
402-471-3121

Nevada
Health Div.
Dept. of Human Services
505 East King Street, Room 600
Carson City, NV 89706
702-687-4740

New Hampshire
Dept. of Health & Human Services
129 Pleasant Street
Concord, NH 03301
603-271-4331

New Jersey
Dept. of Health
John Fitch Plaza., P.O. Box 360
Trenton, NJ 08625
609-292-7837

New Mexico
Dept. of Health
1190 St. Francis Drive
Santa Fe, NM 87504
505-827-2613

New York
Dept. of Health
Corning Tower Building
Empire State Plaza
Albany, NY 12237
518-474-2011

North Carolina
Dept. of Health & Human Services
2001 Mail Service Center
Raleigh, NC 27699
919-733-4534

North Dakota
Dept. of Health
600 East Boulevard Avenue,
  2nd Floor
Bismarck, ND 58505
701-328-2372

Ohio
Dept. of Health
246 North High Street
Columbus, OH 43216
614-466-2253

Oklahoma
State Dept. of Health
1000 N.E. 10th Street
Oklahoma City, OK 73117
405-271-2771

Oregon
Health Services
500 Summer Street, N.E., E-41
Salem, OR 97301
503-947-1175

Pennsylvania
Dept. of Health
P.O. Box 90
Health & Welfare Building
Harrisburg, PA 17108
717-787-6436

Rhode Island
Dept. of Health
3 Capitol Hill
Providence, RI 02908
401-222-2231

South Carolina
Dept. of Health & Human Services
1801 Main Street, P.O. Box 8206
Columbia, SC 29202
803-898-2504

South Dakota
Dept. of Health
600 East Capitol Avenue
Pierre, SD 57501
605-773-3361

Tennessee
Dept. of Health
Cordell Hull Building, 3rd Floor
425 5th Avenue, North
Nashville, TN 37247
615-741-3111

Texas
Dept. of Health
1100 West 49th Street
Austin, TX 78756
512-458-7375

Utah
Dept. of Health
288 North 1460 West
Salt Lake, City, UT 84114
801-538-6111

Vermont
Dept. of Health
108 Cherry Street
Burlington, VT 05402
802-863-7280

Virginia
Dept. of Health
109 Governor Street
Richmond, VA 23219
804-786-3561

Washington
Dept. of Health
P.O. Box 47890
Olympia, WA 98504
360-586-5846

West Virginia
Dept. of Health & Human
  Resources
State Capitol Complex Building 3,
  Room 206
1900 Kanawha Boulevard East
Charleston, WV 25305
304-558-0684

Wisconsin
Dept. of Health & Family Services
P.O. Box 7850
Madison, WI 53702
608-266-0667

Wyoming
Dept. of Health
Hathaway Building, 1st Floor
2300 Capitol Avenue
Cheyenne, WY 82002
307-777-7656

District Of Columbia
Dept. of Health
825 North Capitol Street, N.E.
Washington, DC 20002
202-442-5199

Source: *Directory of Administrative Officials, 2004, published by the Council of State Governments*

G

STATE
LABOR DEPARTMENTS

Following is a list of state agencies that are responsible for administering and enforcing the state's labor laws.

Alabama
Alabama Dept. of Labor
P.O. Box 303500
Montgomery, AL 36130
334-202-3460

Alaska
Dept. of Labor
P.O. Box 21149
Juneau, AK 99801-1149
907-465-2700

Arizona
Industrial Comm.
P.O. Box 19070
Phoenix, AZ 85005-9070
602-542-4515

Arkansas
Dept. of Labor
10421 West Markham, Suite 100
Little Rock, AZ 72205
501-682-4541

California
State Labor Commissioner
455 Golden Gate Avenue, 9th
Floor
San Francisco, CA 94102
415-703-4810

Colorado
Dept. of Labor & Employment
1515 Arapahoe Street
Denver, CO 80202-2117
303-318-8468

Connecticut
Dept. of Labor
200 Folly Brook Boulevard
Wethersfield, CT 06109
860-263-6505

Delaware
Dept. of Labor
4425 North Market Street,
    4th Floor
Wilmington, DE 19802
302-761-6621

Florida
Dept. of Labor
Caldwell Building, Suite 100
107 East Madison Street
Tallahassee, FL 32399
850-245-7105

Georgia
Dept. of Labor
148 International Boulevard, N.E.
Atlanta, GA 30303
404-656-3011

Hawaii
Dept. of Labor & Industrial
    Relations
830 Punchbowl Street, Room 321
Honolulu, HI 96813
808-586-8844

Idaho
Labor & Industrial Services
317 West Main Street
Boise, ID 83735-0001
208-332-3579

Illinois
Dept. of Labor
160 North LaSalle Street,
    Suite C1300
Chicago, IL 60601
312-793-1808

Indiana
Dept. of Labor
IGC-South, Room W195
402 West Washington
Indianapolis, IN 46204-2739
317-232-2738

Iowa
Div. of Labor Services
Dept. of Employment Services
1000 East Grand
Des Moines, IA 50319
515-281-3447

Kansas
Dept. of Human Resources
401 S.W. Topeka Boulevard
Topeka, KS 66603-3182
785-296-7474

Kentucky
Kentucky Dept. of Labor
1047 U.S. 127 South, Suite 4
Frankfort, KY 40601-4381
502-564-3070

Louisiana
Dept. of Labor
P.O. Box 94094
Baton Rouge, LA 70804-9094
225-342-3011

Maine
Dept. of Labor
State House Station #45
Augusta, ME 04333-0045
207-264-6400

Maryland
Div. of Labor & Industry
Dept. of Licensing & Regulation
500 North Calvert Street,
   Suite 401
Baltimore, MD 21202
410-230-6020, ext. 1393

Massachusetts
Dept. of Labor
1 Ashburton Place, Room 2112
Boston, MA 02108
617-727-6573

Michigan
Dept. of Labor
P.O. Box 30004
Lansing, MI 48909
517-373-3034

Minnesota
Dept. of Labor & Industry
443 Lafayette Road
St. Paul, MN 55155
651-284-5010

Mississippi
Dept. of Employment Security
P.O. Box 1699
Jackson, MS 39215-1699
601-321-6100

Missouri
Dept. of Labor & Industrial
   Relations
P.O. Box 599
Jefferson City, MO 65102-0599
573-751-2461

Montana
Dept. of Labor & Industry
P.O. Box 1728
Helena, MT 59624-1728
406-444-9091

Nebraska
Dept. of Labor
P.O. Box 94600
Lincoln, NE 68509
402-471-9000

Nevada
Labor Comm.
555 East Washington Avenue,
   Suite 1400
Las Vegas, NV 89101
702-486-2650

New Hampshire
Dept. of Labor
95 Pleasant Street
Concord, NH 03301
603-271-3171

New Jersey
Dept. of Labor
John Fitch Plaza., P.O. Box 110
Trenton, NJ 08625-0110
609-292-2323

New Mexico
Dept. of Labor
P.O. Box 1928
Albuquerque, NM 87103-1928
505-841-8409

New York
Dept. of Labor
State Office Building #12,
   Room 500
Albany, NY 12240-0003
518-457-2741

North Carolina
Dept. of Labor
4 West Edenton Street
Raleigh, NC 27601-1092
919-733-0359

North Dakota
Dept. of Labor
State Capitol, 6th Floor
600 East Boulevard Avenue,
   Dept. 406
Bismarck, ND 58505-0340
701-328-2660

Ohio
Dept. of Labor Relations
50 West Broad Street, 28th Floor
Columbus, OH 43215
614-644-2239

Oklahoma
Dept. of Labor
4001 North Lincoln Blvd.
Oklahoma City, OK 73105-5212
405-528-1500, ext. 200

Oregon
Bur. of Labor & Industries
800 N.E. Oregon Street, #32
Portland, OR 97232
503-731-4070

Pennsylvania
Dept. of Labor & Industry
Labor & Industry Building,
   Room 1700
7th & Forster Streets
Harrisburg, PA 17120
717-787-5279

Rhode Island
Dept. of Labor
1511 Pontiac Avenue
Cranston, RI 02920
401-462-8870

South Carolina
Dept. of Labor
P.O. Box 11329
Columbia, SC 29211-1329
803-896-4300

South Dakota
Dept. of Labor
700 Governors Drive
Pierre, SD 57501-2291
605-773-3101

Tennessee
Dept. of Labor
710 James Robertson Parkway
Nashville, TN 37243-0655
615-741-6642

Texas
Dept. of Labor Laws
Workforce Employment Comm.
101 East 15th Street, Room 674
Austin, TX 78778
512-463-0735

Utah
State Labor Comm.
P.O. Box 146610
Salt Lake City, UT 84114-6610
801-530-6880

Vermont
Dept. of Labor & Industry
National Life Building
P.O. Drawer 20
Montpelier, VT 05620-3400
802-828-2288

Virginia
Dept. of Labor & Industry
13 South 13th Street
Richmond, VA 23219
804-786-2377

Washington
Dept. of Labor & Industries
P.O. Box 44001
Olympia, WA 98504-4000
360-902-4203

West Virginia
Div. of Labor
State Capitol Complex,
   Building 6, Room B749
Charleston, WV 25305
304-558-7890

Wisconsin
Dept. of Labor & Human
   Relations
P.O. Box 7946
Madison, WI 53707-7946
608-267-9692

Wyoming
Dept. of Employment
1510 East Pershing Boulevard
Cheyenne, WY 82002
307-777-7672

District Of Columbia
Dept. of Employment Services
54 New York Avenue, N.E.,
   Suite 3007
Washington, DC 20002
202-671-1900

Source: *U.S. Dept. of Labor, 2005,*
www.dol.gov.esa

Share the message!

Bulk discounts
Discounts start at only 10 copies and range from 30% to 55% off retail price based on quantity.

Custom publishing
Private label a cover with your organization's name and logo. Or, tailor information to your needs with a custom pamphlet that highlights specific chapters.

Ancillaries
Workshop outlines, videos, and other products are available on select titles.

Dynamic speakers
Engaging authors are available to share their expertise and insight at your event.

Call Kaplan Publishing Corporate Sales at 1-800-621-9621, ext. 4444, or e-mail kaplanpubsales@kaplan.com

PUBLISHING

41081120R00174

Made in the USA
Lexington, KY
28 April 2015